# Osage Avenue

*Coming of Age in the Summer of MOVE*

Tony Gervasi

Riddle Brook Publishing LLC
Peterborough, New Hampshire

Publisher's Cataloging-in-Publication Data
provided by Five Rainbows Cataloging Services

Names: Gervasi, Anthony, author.
Title: Osage Avenue : coming of age in the summer of MOVE / Anthony Gervasi.
Description: Peterborough, NH : Riddle Brook Publishing, 2022.
Identifiers: LCCN 2022937670 (print) | ISBN 979-8-9859413-2-6 (paperback) | ISBN 979-8-9859413-3-3 (ebook)
Subjects: LCSH: African Americans--Pennsylvania—Philadelphia--Biography. | Coming of age. | Police-community relations--Pennsylvania--Philadelphia--History--20th century. | Bombings. | Philadelphia (Pa.)--Race relations. | Africa, John, 1931-1985. | BISAC: BIOGRAPHY & AUTOBIOGRAPHY / Cultural, Ethnic & Regional / African American & Black. | HISTORY / United States / State & Local / Middle Atlantic (DC, DE, MD, NJ, NY, PA)
Classification: LCC F158.9.N4 G47 2022 (print) | LCC F158.9.N4 (ebook) | DDC 974.8--dc23.

Author's Note: *Osage Avenue* is a work of creative nonfiction culled from both fact and memory. While based upon a true story, the events, places, people, and conversations are portrayed only to the best of the author's recollections. In areas where the author was not present or could not have known of the events, conversations, or thoughts that occurred, creative liberties were taken in the service of the overall narrative. Some names, places and minor events have been changed.

Cover Art *Urban Painting Abstract #87* by Mary Ann Reilly
Cover Design by Yosei

ISBN: 979-8-9859413-2-6 (paperback); 979-8-9859413-3-3 (ebook)
LCCN: 2022937670

Riddle Brook Publishing LLC
Peterborough, New Hampshire
www.riddlebrookpublishing.com

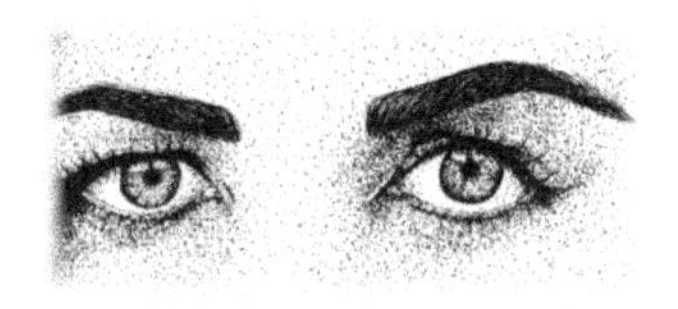

*Valerie*

*The universe is realizing its infinite*
*greatness through your eyes.*
*You are the gateway to its magnificence.*

"Each life is dependent on
every other life, and all life
has purpose."
—*John Africa*

# One

WE ARE BORN INTO CAPTIVITY. SHARON would say an animal born into captivity would have a difficult time surviving anywhere else; it wouldn't know how to get along outside of its cage if it were ever freed. But Smiley said that a captive animal *does* have the instincts to survive outside of its cage.

⁂

Smiley called him Son, or Trey, but his real name was Trigger. He was given the name Trigger because when his mom was nine months pregnant, his dad held a gun to her stomach and tried to shoot him. Whether it was just him, or them, he didn't know. Supposedly the trigger jammed, and instead he just beat the shit out of her with the butt of the gun.

In school Trigger quickly turned into Nigger, then Nee-Gro, which was what most kids called him.

⁂

Over time, the decisions that lead us to our destinies may become distorted in the muddy waters of our brief history, but reflection and loss have the power to bring them to the surface. Some, though, stay safely obscured forever.

In the summer between eighth and ninth grades, Trigger was fourteen, and there was a terrible heat wave blanketing the city of Philadelphia. He lived in West Philadelphia, a concrete-hard area that bred concrete-hard people. Rows of homes tight with frustration, the heat of the day held in by blacktop and limited opportunity.

Because of the uptick in crime, many of the middle-class residents in the neighborhood were moving to the suburbs, creating a void quickly filled with poorer people stepping up from other parts of the city. With this transition, the neighborhood began to slip more into crime, vandalism, and drugs.

At this time, in the mid-1980s, a new drug, powerful and addictive, was creeping its way into the neighborhood of middle class, hardworking people. Crack cocaine brought with it gangs fighting for real estate on which to sell, along with the associated crime and violence. It was pushing out meth, cocaine, and heroin as a cheaper, faster, and better high, but it was still new to many and working to gain a foothold in the city. A lack of good jobs for young people pushed many of them to find other ways to earn a living, and drugs were a fast way to make good money. The older residents took pride in their community, sweeping up the walks in front of their homes and keeping their front porches clean, but the tide of change was difficult to hold back.

⁂

On Monday, May 13, 1985, the day after Mother's Day, a bomb dropped on his neighborhood, and he lay with the animals as his part of the city burned, the whine of sirens beneath their nervous grunts. The dusky smell of smoke drifted for miles, reaching the zoo where he worked and putting the animals on edge, their instincts telling them to run from the flames, but they had no place to go.

He slept in the zoo that night, in the tortoise pen. Backpack pillow. He could hear them scraping along, looking for something, possibly a way out, but there was none. There were a few large boulders they couldn't get behind, and that's where he curled up in the hay. It smelled earthy. Familiar. Hiding from the fire, he was beyond the reach of the problems outside of the pen. Outside of his zoo.

The thing about tortoises is, they live extremely long lives, longer than any other land animal, but most have very small brains. Some don't even have the part of the brain that allows them to feel emotion, which seems to be an advantage if you are going to live longer than anything else. Natural Law has a way of working out the details.

He slept in the zoo a lot of nights. Most nights. But this particular night would be the beginning of a new way of life for him, for everyone in the city. The MOVE people stood their ground, and the city burned with their rage because of it.

Who they were remained a mystery to many, but everyone would find out soon enough. Trigger actually knew more than most people; they lived in his neighborhood, on Osage Avenue. He saw the ramshackle, fortified wooden bunker on their roof. A structure built specifically to resist the threat of authority. The same roof where sweaty hands gripped the cool steel of guns. He saw the loudspeakers on the side of the house. He saw the kids in the street, naked and free and de-evolved. But he didn't know them. Maybe no one outside of the MOVE family really knew them. But he knew *of* them, though he didn't know what was in that boarded-up house, or why. All he knew was something in that house drew him there like a magnet, and he couldn't keep away. He heard that they were primitive, that they fought to remain that way. They looked primitive when he saw them holding protests, demanding freedom for imprisoned people and imprisoned animals. That affected Trigger, their fight for the animals that couldn't fight for themselves.

He was pulled there night after night, caught in the current of fate that flowed down his street and through the turns and dead ends of West Philadelphia, and there was no swimming against it. That house was a beacon for conflict, and people did their best to avoid crashing into it, but those voices called to him and he couldn't resist, just like he couldn't resist living with the animals in the zoo. Just like he couldn't resist the temptation to kill Bob, like Bob had tried to kill him.

# Two

It was the end of April, deep into spring and still a couple of weeks before the bombing, but the nights in his bedroom felt as hot as midsummer. Trigger lay on his mattress, back wet with sweat, and untrimmed hair sticking to his face, the dense brick buildings holding in the heat and frustration of the city. The heat kept Sharon awake too, sagging in her wheelchair. She cracked their bedroom window open for some air, propping it up with a stick left there just for that purpose. Most people open a window for fresh air, but the stale air of the city was all they had, and it carried in the sounds and smells of what flowed on the street below and all the people and animals that were caught in its current. Alley cats and barking dogs penned in on neighbors' porches. Dinners burning along with cigarettes. Loud men laughing and shouting to lonely women wearing too much perfume. Above that blacktop river the words of MOVE blasted through the night, working to smother the chance for anyone who heard it to have thoughts of their own. Those huge speakers near the rooftop bunker vibrated, and MOVE's rage poured out and slid across that river in the street like a fog. It crept into the bedroom that Trigger and Sharon shared, into their heads, as they lay prone to the lashing words.

"You motherfuckers! You're part of the system! You're part of the problem you greedy motherfuckers! Don't you know what the fuck is going on out here! If we can't be free, ain't nobody gonna be free! Nobody's gonna have peace till WE have peace, motherfucker!"

The assault was relentless, and for Sharon it was beyond what she could handle. She pulled herself into bed and rolled and twisted her damaged spine in a futile attempt to find a comfortable place where she could escape into sleep, bending the pillow around her head to muffle the voices. When the heat got too intense, and she couldn't breathe, and her pillow was wet with sweat from her buried face, as wet as the hair sticking to her neck, she broke and climbed back into her chair and wheeled herself into Bob's room at the rear of the house.

There were two bedrooms in the house, theirs in the front and Bob's in the back, and worn oak flooring throughout. In the hall between the rooms was the only bathroom. There was an open banister across from it where the steps led down to the small living room. From the top of the steps, you could see the couch in the living room, and beneath those steps, on the first floor, was a solid wood door that led to the basement.

She woke Bob up, glassy-eyed and hairy, and he plodded down the stairs slow as tar to sleep on the brown couch while she crawled into his bed.

Trigger didn't mind the noise, or what came out of those speakers, but the sound tormented almost every other person in the neighborhood. Tormented them to their limits. He didn't fully understand what they were ranting about, but to him it was a voice somewhere out there looking for someone to hear it, and he did. He could lie back and have those voices rock him to sleep, like a distant lullaby from a mother he didn't know, and who would never get to know him.

❧

Rabbit rabbit.

He was always the first one up, and he was used to getting himself ready for school. Before he got the job at the zoo and starting making his own money, he always grabbed what he could for breakfast in the house, whatever was lying in the kitchen. It was rare to find any fresh food, just maybe some kind of cake or prepackaged food he could eat on his walk. The opposite of MOVE. They only ate raw foods, nothing processed or even cooked.

After he started working, he would usually stop at the corner store and get his own breakfast on the walk.

Trigger liked school and was a good student. It kept him busy, gave him guidance, and he saw how his hard work was rewarded with grades and praise from the teachers. The part he didn't like was the social aspect. The idea of locking all these children together and just expecting them to get along, he didn't understand it, probably because he didn't fit in with the other kids. He was different, and it's easy for groups of the same to single out the one who stands alone. He saw the same thing in the zoo. Animals are put into tight spaces together with no way out, unknown to each other, and are forced to adapt. If not, they are labeled problem animals, even though it wasn't their decision to be there in the first place. In the wild they could just leave and avoid confrontation if they really wanted, but they had no such choice in the zoo, so the strong dominate and create a pack mentality. The pack forces the loner into submission, to follow along with the rest. Trigger didn't have a choice either. He had to be at school. He had to adapt, even though he was considered the outsider for being different. He wasn't the problem animal, but he was the animal that had the problems foisted upon him. So for him, school itself was enough of a social event that he never joined sports or any type of extracurricular activities. He went to school and went home.

He took the long way home from school the next day, just so he could go past the MOVE house. Just so he could see it in the daylight. Things looked different in the light of day, more understandable, less sinister for some reason. Some animals thrive in the dark; some are taught to fear it. He was pulled there gently by an unseen force, just soft enough to keep him feeling secure but strong enough to get him to where it wanted him to go.

There, in the street in front of the home, along with a few dogs that looked stray, were some of the MOVE children. They were easy to spot. Dreadlocks, like the rest, some wearing clothes, but a few smaller ones as naked as when they were brought into the world. Right there, right in West Philadelphia, naked children in the street. Re-wilding. De-evolution. They didn't go to school. School was part of the system, and they were not to be contaminated by the system.

One of the older kids there was a girl about Trigger's age. She was stamping her feet and clapping her hands in rhythm to a song only she heard. She was smiling and looked so content moving to that song no one else heard that he stopped and found himself smiling with her. She didn't talk to him, and he didn't know her, but she was infectious in a way that forced him to recognize the beautiful spring day, forced him to acknowledge his environment. Somehow that smile, that energy, cut through him like a live wire had fallen at his feet and shocked him awake. He later found out her name was Tree Africa, her last name the same as everyone who followed John

Africa. She lived in that house, with the words from the speakers so close to her ear she couldn't hide her head in a pillow.

Like the children in the MOVE house, his sister Sharon didn't go to school anymore either. Bob had pulled her out three years earlier, when she was Trigger's age, between eighth and ninth grades. She was different than Trigger was when she was his age, almost the opposite. She wasn't a good student. Learning didn't come naturally for her. Things that seemed easy for others were difficult for her. She had a case of dyslexia that was not diagnosed until much later in life, and when she couldn't understand or comprehend the assignments, and couldn't get help to figure it out, she got frustrated and began to hate schoolwork. Her grades consistently trended downward, and the worse they got the worse her attitude became. She was labeled slow, difficult, and lazy. And the more she was labeled, the angrier and more humiliated she became. She started to resent the friends she had, more than she already did, as they could run and play and dance while she could only watch from her chair. Soon she had distanced herself from everyone. After constantly complaining about school to Bob, the easiest thing to do, he decided, was to just have her leave and be home-schooled. It was a decision she regretted almost immediately, but going back was not an option. Bob had gotten her on disability as well, and the checks he received became habit; he wouldn't give that up easily.

She spent all day in the house, a brick rowhouse in the middle of a block of others, in a city of millions of brick rowhouses, the body of each separated from the others by cinder, some having a back porch with only thinner plywood walls providing privacy, dividing neighbor from neighbor.

Sharon shared the front bedroom with Trigger while Bob had the rear room. Back then they just called him Dad, but everybody else called him Big Bob. They moved there after their mom died, killed in a car crash when Trigger was six and Sharon nine. They were both in the car; he got a scar across the forehead to remember it by, Sharon got a wheelchair. Trigger felt it was his fault their mom had died and his fault Sharon was paralyzed, and he carried that with him everywhere, like a second shadow he was terrified of.

She spent the schooldays with Bob on the couch, together in their pain, growing closer. Uncomfortably close, Trigger thought. He never actually saw them doing any kind of studying, but he wasn't there most of the day. By the time he got home from school or the zoo they'd just be on that couch, spending hours together. When Bob would finally pull his massive frame up off the couch, he would groan and stretch, then wash down another oxycodone with his beer, numbing the pain in his back, old football injury he used to say, but who knows. He would lumber into the basement like a tired gorilla and turn on some music, and Trigger would take his place on the couch. That soft couch.

Bob and Sharon leaned on each other, lamenting poor decisions and the indifference of fate. The more time they spent on that couch, separated from society, the more they began to believe that it was all they deserved. All they could ever achieve. And that only added to the pain, and the more pain they felt the more they needed to deaden it. It was a whirlpool sucking them down, and the ride gave them some comfort, but the deeper they got the harder it was to swim against.

After a while the pills stopped working fast enough, and Bob started crushing them and snorting up the powder and sharing with Sharon. When that wasn't enough to numb them, to help them forget, they turned to more potent and addictive methods.

It creeps up slowly, addiction, and is rarely noticed in oneself until it's too late to corral it. Weeks pass, then months, then most of a lifetime.

Bob didn't have friends, which Trigger and Sharon didn't find strange, because they didn't have any either, and none of them, none of the three of them, ever had people over to the house. That was why Trigger thought it unusual when he came back from the zoo one night and Bob was sitting on the porch with another man. Younger than Bob, he looked familiar. Familiar in a way like there were dozens of him, people like him, all over the neighborhood. They smoked cigarettes and talked like they had known each other for years, and maybe they had. They were still talking out front when Sharon and Trigger went to bed, and their voices carried up to their window, loud enough so she had to roll out and sleep in the rear bedroom, Bob's room. Trigger had no place to go, and the next morning was a Saturday and he had to work. The voices kept him up all night but not like the frustrated, unwavering bluster from the MOVE house; these closer voices carried only meaningless chatter.

The next day the man was still at the house. Trigger's house. He was sleeping comfortably on the couch, while Trigger had been forced to drag himself to work exhausted and late. Fatigue would soon become a relentless nemesis.

It was the first time he'd been late, and by the time he made it to Smiley's office, the rest of the maintenance crew had already been sent out on their assignments for the day. Everyone called him Smiley, but his name was Sam. He called himself Uncle Sam and asked everyone to call him uncle too, but Trigger only called him Smiley. He didn't want Smiley to be part of his family.

Smiley had worked at the zoo for over twenty years and probably knew more about the animals than the vets taking care of them. He had seen animals born in the zoo and die in the zoo, some never seeing the outside of their pens or cages in their entire lifetimes. Tall and bone thin, he was angular and dark, his tan button-down shirt hanging loose and billowing out. Blacker than most blacks, laughing while saying he was double-dipped. His deep-set eyes had lines in the corners from years of laughter, and he was always smiling. He would smile just looking at the sky or if he was shoveling shit, it didn't matter to him, it all seemed good. Maybe it was because he had one of those big smiles, where you could see all the way to his yellowing back teeth. A smile everyone wanted but few possessed. A smile Trigger could only wish to someday have.

"Early is on time, on time is late, and late is trouble, son."

Even when he tried to be stern, he did it with a smile. It was just his nature.

"Let me tell you a couple things . . ." He held out his left pinkie and struck it with that long leathery index finger of his right hand, then moved down a finger with each point he made. "It don't cost nothing to be polite." Pinkie. "It don't cost nothing to help somebody when they need it." Ring finger. "And it don't cost not a damn thing to be on time." Middle finger.

"You remember that, you got no worries, my son."

He took a deep breath in through his flat nose, and his thin chest filled, then relaxed.

"You got a watch?"

Trigger shook his head no.

Smiley slid open his desk drawer and dug around.

"Here," he held out a black, rubber Casio watch. "Found this last week. The band is broken, but it'll keep you on time just the same."

Trigger looked from the watch to Smiley's dark eyes, then back to the watch.

"Well," Smiley said, "Watchu waiting for? Go on. Take it."

Trigger snatched it quickly from the man's wide, creased palm and stuffed it into his pocket.

Smiley sent Trigger off on trash duty, where he spent the afternoon with his animal family. When his shift was over, he stayed until the zoo closed. Trigger loved the zoo and, if he could have, would have made it his home. He was lucky enough to work there, spending as much time there as possible, but like everything else in his life, it came with a struggle.

It was during a school trip. As kids drifted along the paths under the lazy eye of their young teacher, a few of the more brazen ones broke off on their own, Trigger among them. Not that he was a part of the group, he was just drawn away by the sounds and smells, each exhibit taking him to different areas of the world. He ended up at the African Plains exhibit, he at one end of the habitat, and the small group of his classmates at the other. The first stone was thrown by the most rebellious and obnoxious kid, Will Thomas, who would come to factor into Trigger's life in many ways.

After that first toss, it was easy for the others to follow. They worked at pelting a small zebra. Not a full-grown adult quite yet but not a baby either. They snickered, looking down the path to be sure no one was watching them as they did their best to pepper it with handfuls of gravel and any larger stones they could come across. If they got lucky and hit it, the zebra's fur would quiver, as if getting stung by a bee. It would walk off to avoid another sting, but the boys would follow it, laughing and trying again. As they laughed, Trigger held in his anger for as long as he could. He didn't want to get involved, he knew the danger in that.

Stone to animal. Each time it kicked and shook with the sting, the boys would laugh and Trigger would tamp down his frustration. It couldn't defend itself, so he finally took the risk and shouted for them to stop. Will turned a side eye to Trigger and strutted over with three other boys following. Words were exchanged, then Will shoved Trigger. He returned the shove, then was popped in the eye with a bony fist, then another. Trigger fought back hard, as best he could, but he was outmatched and got pummeled for doing what he thought was right. Will eventually got him into a tight headlock, where he could wrench Trigger's neck and laugh toward the other boys while at the same time Trigger unsuccessfully struggled to break free.

"Say it Nee-Gro!" Will shouted, almost laughing as he tightened his bony forearm into Trigger's neck.

"Say Will's your Daddy! Say I'm sorry, Daddy!"

The other boys laughed, and the more they laughed the more Will wrestled him around by the neck. Just as Trigger was about to give in and say what he needed to be set free, to admit he was the weaker one, a large set of hands reached in and worked at prying Will off.

"Hey, hey hey . . . break it up now."

Smiley had witnessed the whole thing, and by the time he pulled Will off, Trigger was red in the face and breathing hard, teeth clenched. He turned his back to wipe the tears from his face.

"You boys go on and get."

Smiley sent the other boys on their way and walked with Trigger to find the rest of his class. During the walk, Smiley told Trigger he was going to give him three free passes to the zoo, just for doing what was right. And that was fine by Trigger.

Each time he used one of the passes, he stayed until the zoo closed, and each time he went, he found Smiley, or Smiley found him. Smiley eventually offered him a part-time job, just a few hours a week at first, and Trigger jumped at the chance. A chance to get closer to the animals. He wondered how the animals acted at night, when no people were around and all they heard were each other's sounds, and the world was theirs again, and they struggled to understand the limitations of their environment. He would find out.

Trigger checked the watch Smiley had given him. It was the first time he had ever owned a watch. His shift was over, but he stayed until the zoo closed, then left by the service gate in the rear of the zoo. There were different gates on Zoological Drive, the service road behind the zoo. Each gate served as access for zoo workers. There was the hospital gate, the commissary gate, the grounds crew gate, and the service gate. The zoo ran north to south, pressed between the Schuylkill River and West Philadelphia, and directly across from Zoological Drive were train tracks. The Victorian entrance with its heavy iron gates was at the north end. In the center of the zoo was a large lake, then to the east the African exhibit, otters, and prairie dogs. To the west were the big cats, elephants, and the petting zoo. In between were lots of other buildings: exhibits and stolen lives. Overall the zoo covered more than forty acres.

Trigger walked up the drive to 34th Street and to the bridge that would bring him back to his neighborhood. The Schuylkill River carved its way through the city, isolating West Philadelphia, and on the east side of the river was Boathouse Row, with brightly lit boathouses where the fortunate people spent their days on the water rowing their worries away. Not far from that (and a world away from West Philadelphia) was the Philadelphia Art Museum, then North Philadelphia, South Philadelphia, Rittenhouse Square, and Center City, where droves of tourists huddled around the Liberty Bell, the national symbol of freedom, which lay far enough from the zoo that the animals didn't know about it. All were places unknown to Trigger, full of other lives that were mysteries to him. His reality was this neighborhood, the one that included Osage Avenue, the one within walking distance of the zoo, the only thing that really mattered to him these days.

The walk from his house to the zoo took about an hour, and every hour he walked it he spent asking himself questions he was too young to answer, and every time he walked it he felt more and more alone.

The soothing undercurrent of fate carried him back to Osage Avenue, back to the MOVE house. Living on the cusp of darkness, the street hummed with hidden lives and the static in the speakers on the MOVE house. A voice crackled from it, waking up any animals that were asleep.

"Get ready for a long night, cause it's gonna be a long goddamn night!"

The sun set, but the air seemed to stay just as hot. People locked themselves inside to escape the voice blasting from those speakers, but Trigger sat on a cool concrete stoop across the street and listened to the insistent voice he heard each night, coming from the rooftop bunker of the MOVE house, the voice that seemed to speak to him alone. It cursed at him, how he was an ignorant motherfucker, how everyone was. How the fuck didn't he understand what was going on? How was everyone a part of this rotten government system? It raged about the brothers and sisters they wanted freed, the nine who, less than a decade earlier had all been found guilty, even without evidence, for the death of a cop, and how no one would have peace until they were released. Not just none of them on that street, or in that neighborhood, or in that city, but no one.

Trigger didn't understand what they meant, or who they were in that house and in that rooftop bunker, but it felt like something was happening in there, like it was a pot of water set on a flame, and right now the water was calm and warm, almost inviting, but the hotter it got the more turbulent and dangerous that water became. He didn't know who lit the fire or why, but he could feel the heat, like something was about to boil over into the street and then it would be everyone's problem to deal with, not just the burden of the people inside. Something in that house was trying to make change.

There were changes in his house happening too. A different kind of fire. Changes in Bob and Sharon. She was in their room less often when he woke up, but it was never talked about with Trigger as to why. She spoke to Trigger less often. Distant. A few times in the morning, Bob wasn't on the couch when she was in his room. And Bob had fastened a thick deadbolt on the basement door, the kind you would see on a big industrial garage door, with a heavy brass padlock. He spent hours in the basement, working on perfecting his poison. Creating and feeding an addiction and hoping to find a shortcut to making an easy living while at it. The man who sat on the porch and slept on the couch taught him how.

There was only one meth lab in the neighborhood, on Osage Avenue, and Bob didn't want to be forced to rely on anyone for his fix. Once he learned how to make it himself, he kept the secret locked up in the basement. The key hung from a chain around his neck. It was there for everyone to see because he rarely bothered to put a shirt on any longer, shoes either. And Sharon never seemed to change her clothes. They both stayed on that couch, him shirtless and her in the same dirty clothes, for days at a time, and Trigger was the only one using the bathroom to take showers.

One morning as he got himself ready for school, he squeezed the last bit of toothpaste out of the tube, folding it again and again to get at the final pea-sized drop. Downstairs he showed Bob, the crumpled tube in his flat palm.

"We're out of toothpaste."

Bob nodded his head, eyelids drooping.

Trigger waited, but the nod was all he got out of him.

"Dad . . . we're out of toothpaste," he said again. "Can you get some today?"

Bob held his hand up and gave the okay signal, eyes like a basset hound, and it seemed to take all of his energy just to do that.

"I got it," he said, but the next morning there was no new toothpaste. Trigger brushed his teeth with water, still tasting a bit of leftover mint in the bristles. He asked again, and again Bob said he would take care of it.

No toothpaste the next morning either.

Seems like a small thing, no toothpaste for a few days. But days turned into a week and there was still no toothpaste. Back and forth this went until Trigger faced the fact that there would be no new toothpaste unless he bought it. Same with soap. When he used it up, it wasn't replaced. When a bulb burned out in his room, he searched the house to find one but couldn't. His room simply got darker.

To the brown couch.

"I need some money, Dad," he said. "I need some money to get some stuff. Toothpaste, and soap and light bulbs and stuff."

Both Bob and Sharon were glued to that couch, not concerned about toothpaste or soap or light bulbs, or their place in the universe.

"A light bulb is like a dollar," Bob chuckled. "You got a job. You got a dollar. Go get a light bulb if you want one. It's about time you started carrying your own weight around here anyway."

"You should buy the stuff. Sharon needs stuff too. And there's nothing to eat in the kitchen."

Bob strained to lean forward, and with great effort slid his beer off the table, then leaned back and took a slug, winking as he tipped the can up, then let out a wet burp.

"You got some money. Go get it."

Trigger shook his head. He shoveled shit in the zoo for what little he had, and it didn't feel right to him. He kicked the leg of the table.

"This ain't fair. It ain't fair I gotta spend my money on stuff for the house."

"Fair!"

Bob erupted like he had been waiting to hear those words for years, just so he could explode and release what was boiling under his skin.

He whipped his beer can past Trigger and into the wall. Trigger ducked, but it wasn't close to hitting him. He had never seen Bob flip like that so fast, and his eyes got wide and blood pushed fast through his thin body. Sharon pushed herself as far to the end of the couch as she could with almost all of the little strength she had.

"What the hell you know about fair? Life ain't fair. You're gonna bitch about toothpaste? About light bulbs?"

"Jesus," Sharon said, with a lazy drawl that took the rest of her energy. "Relax."

Bob ran his fingers through his wiry hair and took a hard breath out, then laughed out loud, shaking his head.

Trigger could have gone on. He could have gone on about how there was beer in the house, and pills, and an endless supply of cigarettes, and how he was just a kid, and how Bob was supposed to be the adult and provide the toothpaste. He wanted to go on, and he felt rebellion bubbling up inside, making him tense and uncomfortable, but he didn't. He couldn't. It wasn't fair.

That was the first time he felt that feeling. That feeling that he was on his own, alone. No guiding force, no breakfast waiting on the table, or family pets to roll around with, or haircuts on the porch from a proud mother.

How the fuck didn't Bob understand what was going on? Maybe, he thought, Bob was the problem.

Something echoed in his head, like the reverb from a speaker.

Later that night, when Bob was decomposing on the couch, Trigger sneaked into his room, heart pumping as the creak of the door threatened to wake the dead. On the dresser was a crumpled-up pile of small bills. Trigger smoothed out a five for toothpaste and light bulbs. He slid it in his pocket and brushed up against the watch Smiley gave him, making him pause and consider both men. He didn't even make it out of the room before he wrinkled the bill back up in his fist and returned it. He bought the toothpaste with his own money.

He kept the cash that he made from the zoo stashed in the strap of his backpack, slicing a small slit into it so he could roll up the bills and keep them safely hidden away. It was always with him, and as safe a place as he could think to keep it.

Trigger was still sleeping in the house every night, although he was getting used to finding his own food and taking care of himself. Clothes stunk like the zoo cages and needed to be dealt with, but the washing machine was in the basement, and Bob had bolted that lock on the door. The first time he asked if he could go down and do laundry, which he had no idea how to do, Bob just said no, without explaining more. The next time he asked, Bob snapped, just like with the toothpaste.

"Your clothes are clean enough. I don't want you going down there no more."

"What do you mean clean enough? My clothes are dirty, I have to wash them, same with Sharon. She's been wearing the same clothes all the time."

"Don't you worry about her, she's just fine. You too, your clothes are fine. If you're that worried about it, go to the laundromat at the end of the block."

Trigger held his hands up and shook his head, mouth open and hair brushing into his eyes.

"Laundromat? We have a washer right down there. Why can't we just . . ."

"I said no, goddammit. No going down there, what don't you understand about that? My house, my rules."

He didn't know how to do laundry at a laundromat. He didn't even know how to do it in a house, but carrying a bunch of clothes down the street and trying to figure that out, it was daunting to him.

Later that week he *did* carry his clothes, bundled in arms, down the street, stooping and picking up what dropped every few yards. By the following week he had a bag with both his clothes and Sharon's. He bought soap there and sat as the machines rolled and the old black ladies from the neighborhood complained about that boarded-up house with the people yelling, and the rhythm of the machines and warm perfume-scented air lulled him into a comfortable place. He did laundry and had clean clothes to wear and was content.

The same man who was on the porch keeping him up was at the house more often. He became a fixture and began to bring other people with him. It got to the point where they no longer knocked on the door, they just came in. If Trigger was on that brown couch and the door opened, he sprang up the steps and locked himself in the bedroom. Sometimes Sharon would stay down there with them, sometimes she would be in Bob's room.

The line between which bedroom was Sharon's was beginning to blur, Bob's or the front room she'd been sharing for so long with Trigger.

Music cranked all night and even drowned out the loudspeakers from the MOVE house, drifting through the smoke's haze. They brought crack, and Bob shared his meth with them, hoping to create a demand. It became too much one night. Trigger's room was holding in the heat of the day, and the noise from the music and the voices downstairs swirled around him like a tempest, to the point where he wrapped his head in a shirt to muffle it, but it didn't work. It was too hot. Stuffing some clothes into his backpack he went to leave, walking right by the couch. Bob sat there with two rail-thin men looking near death.

It was late, and Bob yelled for him to get back upstairs. Trigger started to head back up, but by the time he made it to the steps he saw Bob take a huge hit off a pipe, hard enough so that he coughed and the red-hot crystals shot out onto the dark wood floor. The other guys laughed, then Bob laughed. They all sat there on that couch, laughing as Trigger watched like a ghost in the shadows. He walked right by them then, and all three ignored him as he floated out the door, invisible.

It was the latest he had ever been outside, and it seemed like it was as dark as the universe had ever been, and he didn't even know where he was going. It didn't matter, the river of the street knew where it wanted him to be. Back to the MOVE house.

At the MOVE house, the speakers on the house were quiet and nothing could be seen through the small slats of the rooftop bunker. If not for the bunker on the roof and all of the boarded-up windows, it might have passed for any other regular house on the street.

But it wasn't just another house on the street. It was a fortification. A structure built for defiance, slowly assembled over many months. From plywood. From fallen tree logs. From corrugated metal. Ramps built. Openings sealed. It was a revolution growing in the belly of the brick walls. A seed of disdain and frustration taking root, preparing for the heavy leather boot heel coming to crush it out.

Trigger didn't understand these things at the time, he just knew something different was going on in there, and he wondered if Tree Africa knew what it was. She was no older than him. They lived in the same area, under the same moon, and both had to eat and sleep and knock into problems and questions, but she had to know more than he did, and he was unsure if that was good or not.

When he went back to his own house, voices still rumbled from inside, on the couch, his couch, so he waited, sitting on the porch. There was a cut of leftover carpeting between him and the cool concrete, and he laid down on it. He was so tired and had to be up for school the next day. He slipped the backpack under his heavy head.

Backpack pillow. It was the first night—but far from the last—that Trigger slept outside.

⁂

That cold, rusted grill headed for him like it did every night, angry and looking to take it out on someone. Then the screaming and the heat.

⁂

Rabbit rabbit.

He woke up stiff, just that thin remnant of rug for padding, sore and bone-tired from a night on the porch, too sore for a boy of that age. Inside was one of the dead still on the couch, propped up like a sickly puppet. Alive, but not living. The world was littered with them, each with their own excuses and ghosts, teetering on the edge of nothingness. Dead to everything except what filled the void they created in themselves, and this one was in his house.

Beer cans, pipes, spoons, and baggies all on the coffee table for the universe to see. Peeking out from beneath a baggie was a needle. Upstairs, Bob's bedroom door was open and Sharon's chair sat empty inside. She was in his bed, and he was in there too, her under the covers and him on top but close together on the small mattress.

Dragging and foggy, Trigger was too tired to figure it all out. He got himself cleaned up as best he could and began the walk to school.

Directly across the street, watering some plants in the morning sun on her porch, was an older woman, skin dark and creased. She wore a light, ankle-length housedress, white and clean, as white as the short curly hair on her head. Her face was framed with cat eyeglasses, and she looked at Trigger, tipping up the watering can for a moment. She smiled and gave a short wave of her hand. Trigger stopped for just a second and wondered if she knew what was going on in his house. If she heard the music, or the talking, or the yelling. He ignored her and went on his way, wanting only to get back to the zoo.

# Three

THE SUMMER INCHED CLOSER, AND IT WAS going to be stifling. Trigger felt it on the back of his sweaty neck when he woke up. He could hear it in the words spewing across the neighborhood like lava from those speakers, and he could taste it on his tongue, like the first time he tasted the fumes from the basement.

Bob had been spending hours down there, working on his craft. Sometimes someone would be with him and music would rattle the house, but mostly Bob worked alone. He didn't try to hide his drug use any longer, not that he'd tried all that hard to begin with. Trigger knew that Bob had completely given up when Trigger pushed the front door open one day after school—day, not night—and walked in from the outside world to see, there on the couch, next to what looked like a skinny black corpse of a man, Bob, shirtless, belt tight around his arm, veins plump and rising to the surface of his skin, and watched as the needle plunged into his vein while he looked up and saw Trigger, not caring. Bob saw Trigger and all of his youth and all of his future. He squinted into Trigger's sunlight-washed silhouette and Trigger looked back at him in the darkness, into what Bob had created for himself. Trigger turned to look away but it was too late. He saw, and Bob saw, and the universe saw, and nothing could ever change that. Bob laid back with a groan, head knocking against the wall, and closed his eyes.

Trigger never wanted to sit on that comfortable couch again.

As the weeks dragged on, more people started drifting into the house and hanging around the porch and stoop. It got to the point where there was so much going on, even sleeping on the porch was impossible. Trigger spent a few nights just wandering, somehow always drifting past that house on Osage Avenue. An entire night could go by and he wouldn't even know where he had been, then he would collapse back in his room after the dead had cleared out. Always so tired. A few times he was so exhausted he passed out on the stoop across from the MOVE house, the words from the loudspeaker sometimes shouting at him, sometimes silent, sleeping sitting up, waiting for someone or something to tell him what to do.

At least he could leave. When things got uncomfortable, he had an escape. Sharon was at the mercy of her chair and the stairs, and Trigger believed it was his fault. It was unjust, as many things are, but through injustice change can occur. It's what MOVE called *The Duration of the Struggle*. As much time as it took to cause an issue, that much time was needed to undo it. The larger the injustice, the longer to rectify. Some might take centuries to undue, if that was the length of time sacrificed to create the injustice itself.

Sharon was sleeping in Bob's room almost every night now, explaining to Trigger that it was because of the noise from the street, the noise from the MOVE house, but he was able to sleep through it just fine now, which left him skeptical. He'd gotten used to it. More than avoiding the noise, he thought, she was trying to elude her life, to ignore the path she was on, no longer fighting the current, just taken by it, and she did this by getting high, smoking meth in that room. She would wheel her chair across the hall and look down into the darkness and see who was on the couch, then back into Bob's room or into their room. What used to be their room. What seemed was now just Trigger's room. She drifted back and forth in her own world, still in her same clothes. He'd bought the toothpaste but was the only one using it.

He'd caused the accident, though; he'd changed the path. If not for him, he assumed, her life would be completely different. Stable. Not hanging from its hinges.

Bob seemed more unhinged as well. When Sharon spent a night in Trigger's room, he insisted on knowing why.

"What do you mean, Dad? It's her room too."

"Bob."

"What?"

"Just Bob. Just call me Bob."

And that was that. He was now just Bob.

There was never an explanation as to why he was now just Bob, but he was, and would be from that point on, and with it, Bob gave himself one less responsibility.

To answer his own question—why Sharon was in the front bedroom she shared with Trigger—Bob decided to pull off the front bedroom door and stack it on the porch in the unkempt backyard. Paranoia began to whisper through his foggy mind, and he relented to its demands. Soon after that, he pulled off his own bedroom door too, ensuring Sharon hid nothing from him and exposing his own secrets at the same time.

A few days later, when Trigger came home from school and

found even the bathroom door gone, he started to feel that things were spiraling. He had seen animals go to the bathroom all the time at the zoo and was usually the one who had to clean it up, but an animal doesn't know shame. An animal isn't taught that it's disgusting or embarrassing: It eats, and what it eats comes out again. He wondered if, were he never taught differently, would it matter who he went to the bathroom in front of? How would he know it was wrong? He wouldn't know, and it wouldn't matter, but he was taught, and it was wrong. Evolved. There was no door on the bathroom and that wasn't normal, that much he *did* know. The animals in the zoo didn't have doors either. He wondered if Tree Africa had a door on her room. Or lights. Or toothpaste.

❧

The closer summer got, the more Trigger wanted to stay at the zoo. Smiley was spending almost every lunch break with him. He was always tired, Smiley saw that in him. Trigger tried his best, but his clothes were still dirty, almost as dirty as his body, and Smiley saw that as well but never said anything about it. He didn't ask Trigger any questions, but he had a way of hinting at things around their work. Like after he cleaned out the orangutan exhibit once. They were having their break at the picnic bench like usual, Smiley leaning back in the sun with that wide smile, smiling just at his own thoughts.

"How'd you make out today, cleaning out that cage?"

Before Trigger even had a chance to answer he continued, like he was just bringing it up to get to another point.

"Those orangutans, they interesting all right. You know, there's one out in San Diego Zoo; second best zoo in the country by the way . . . there's one out there they call Harry Houdini. He escaped out his cage! Bunch of times! Can you believe that? Right outta his cage . . . orangutan figuring a way out. Yeah, guess he don't like it so much in there."

He pulled his hat off and scratched at his tight cut hair and winked at Trigger. "You believe that? Sometimes I guess things so bad he just gotta get out. Not like he can ask nobody for help, he's just an animal, you know. You know what I'm getting at?"

Trigger leaned back up against a tree in the shade, where he always sat. "Yeah, that's weird," was all he said. But he *did* know what Smiley was getting at, or at least he thought he did.

The more time Trigger spent with Smiley, the more hours he was given, and that was fine with him. He liked being there, and at first he thought maybe Smiley just needed more help, but he began to understand maybe someone was looking out for him a bit.

The zoo had a large storage shed where they kept hay for all the animals, and they went through a lot of hay. Later in his shift one day, right before the heat of summer was getting ready to cloak the city, Trigger was cleaning up the shed and sat down on a hay bale. It was so warm out, and he was so tired. His sitting became lying back, and he stretched out his spine and gave his legs a needed rest. It was so comfortable, but he didn't want to be seen lying down, so he got up and crawled to the bales in back of the shed, out of sight. So tired.

He was so exhausted he didn't even dream the grill of the truck, just the warm blackness of nothing.

When he woke up it was dark, the zoo was empty of people and lights and noise; the only sounds to be heard were the animals talking to each other. He wandered the lamplit paths, wandered the grass and the trees, and selfishly whispered to the animals about his issues, unwittingly neglecting theirs. The moon followed over his shoulder, and his shadow stretched out like a spindly spider across the paths and into the cages with the other animals. Not drawing him to where it wanted him to go like the river of fate on Osage

Avenue; instead it walked as a partner, careless as Trigger led the way. With the moon and the dark night and the smell of the hay and the light dew on the grass, there was a quiet beauty that only he and the animals could witness, and he wished he could magically transport Sharon there to breathe it in with them. Drifting free in the moment, without the worry of what lay ahead or of memories past. Free in the beauty of the world and an endless universe of possibilities. Free in a zoo of prisoners.

By the time he saw a night security guard, he had almost forgotten about the world outside the zoo. Almost, but the guard snapped him back into West Philadelphia. Trigger spotted him first, so he was able to hide in the shadows, cramming himself between some barrels and the fence that separated him from the wolves in their enclosure. Close enough that he could pretend to be an animal but still safely beyond the wolves' reach. He sat and thought of how he could get out. All the gates were locked, and the fence surrounding the zoo had razor wire at the top.

He was pinned in but not trapped. Smiley had master keys to all the locks, and Trigger decided he was going to get one. He would get one not only to get out but to get in. He sat in the heat behind those barrels, just him and the moon and the wolves, and fell back asleep. He was even beyond the voices that called to him from Osage Avenue.

# Four

THE NEIGHBORHOOD PEOPLE WERE MAKING their voices heard. Maybe not as loud and angry as MOVE, but they were not just shouting into the night. No, they were going to the people who could do something. To city hall and to the authorities that MOVE was raging against, just as MOVE had hoped they would. If they irritated the neighbors enough, MOVE thought, without breaking any laws, the people would have to go to the authorities for help. It would be then that MOVE would use their position and power to their advantage, demanding the release of their nine incarcerated brothers and sisters who had been jailed since 1978. So they tormented the neighbors to the brink of legality, then pulled back each night, killing the speakers just before the noise curfew kicked in. The neighbors who heard those speakers spewing out venom, sometimes naming people on the street, disgorging directed threats, who saw the windows as they were boarded up and the rooftop bunker as it was built, and the dreadlocks and children and axes, they had seen enough. Many had worked their way up to Osage Avenue from other areas in the city much worse off, areas that some people called slums, worked up to what was supposed to be a gentler and more promising way of life, and it was threatened now by the voices behind those speakers. From two in the afternoon until two in the morning, the speakers rattled the neighbors with MOVE's philosophy, angry and threatening to anyone opposed to them. But people had to be at work in the morning, and they couldn't get a solid night's sleep. MOVE's neighbors were exhausted with a war they had no stake in and had nothing to gain from. They'd gone to the police and even the mayor, but the city had done nothing, had actively avoided the situation. And they just wanted their lives back to normal.

Roaches, rats, and other vermin, drawn first by the garbage piled up outside of the MOVE house and the raw meat thrown to dozens of stray dogs, began working their way through the neighborhood, people fighting uselessly against the tide. One neighbor stopped her children playing in their own front yard. Another let the oven run for half an hour to make sure all the vermin had scattered before cooking her casseroles. And as time went on, their situation became more desperate. Children playing in the street would hear the vicious profanity day after day, building a thick skin, and with impunity used the words they'd heard. Parents did their best to keep them indoors, but it was the beginning of summer, the warm air called to them. The transition was slow at first, but now something had to be done. A compromise was needed, and if a compromise couldn't be reached, that pot was going to boil over and scald the whole city—and the fire under it was going to burn wild.

The neighbors held protests themselves, called for news conferences, anything to bring light to their struggle.

They promised the new mayor, Wilson Goode, the city's first Black mayor, that if he didn't solve the problem then they would. The standoff on Osage Avenue was coming to a head.

No compromise would be reached, and the neighbors reached out to the governor.

⁂

After that first unintentional night in the zoo, Trigger did what he thought he could never do: He planned to steal from Smiley. He needed to walk with the moonlight again and drift through the beauty he perceived in the same way Bob must have wanted his fix. A temporary solution to a larger problem but one that felt good, one that meant not having to deal with bigger issues for a while.

He wanted the master key.

It took about a week, and it really wasn't difficult. Smiley simply kept the spare master keys in the pencil drawer of his desk, beneath the pencil tray. Trigger caught it one morning when a maintenance worker said the cashier at the snack shack had accidentally locked her keys in the building at closing the day before. He asked Smiley for a master key, and he slid that drawer out, lifted the tray and handed it over, and then Trigger knew. There were no reservations to pulling it out in front of him; that's how much Smiley trusted. Smiley held that key by the teeth and raised it up to his eye, looking through the bow hole at the worker. Smiley was just about as serious as he was able to be.

"You don't come back with this, it's coming out of yo' check, not mine."

The next day at lunch, as Smiley basked in the sun, Trigger crept off into his office and slid that drawer out, slow and stealthy as a cat. Right behind Smiley's beaming face, he stabbed him in his dark, bony back with that key. It seemed like it was glowing white hot, so hot that it burnt his fingertips to where he fought to hold onto it, where he wanted so badly to let go and put it back, but Natural Law doesn't rule with emotion. He jammed that key in his pocket and closed the drawer. De-evolution.

Although he stole the key and now had total access to the zoo, he didn't spend a night there for a while. He was afraid. Afraid not only of getting caught and what Smiley would think of him, but afraid if he crossed that boundary and purposely spent the night in the zoo with the animals, he would be starting down a path difficult to return from. It was an idea that he didn't entirely think through, stealing the key; not that many ideas fourteen-year-old kids have are well thought out. If he didn't use it and just slipped it back into the desk, it would be like he never took it at all, and he would be the only one who would ever know of the betrayal. Sometimes there is no harsher judge of immoral deeds than the one who has perpetrated them. But he kept it. He had a small yellow change purse that snapped shut, and he tucked that key away, and he felt it burning in his back pocket all summer, as valuable to him as the key on that chain tightening around Bob's neck.

By late spring it was already broiling out, and everyone was irritated with sweat and frustration, and Bob retreated into the cool basement to make supplies for the dead. Trigger could taste the fumes when he came in from the heavy summer air, stale and sour on the tip of his tongue, like the taste of ammonia in the air of a hospital. Bob was his own barometer, testing everything, and his drug consumption slowly overtook him, like a parasite working on him from the inside.

There's a certain type of wasp that attacks orb spiders. Stings and paralyzes them, then injects an egg into the spider's abdomen. When the spider wakes up, it doesn't even realize it has the egg and goes about its normal life. When the egg hatches, the larva attaches to the spider and feeds off it, and when its ready to transition to an adult, it releases a chemical into the spider that controls its nervous system. The spider then reconstructs its web to what would best suit the larva's cocoon. When the web is done, the zombie spider waits in the center, it waits to be killed. The larva, when ready, sucks the life out of its slave, making its cocoon right where the spider made it the safest, and eventually a full-grown wasp emerges and begins its own life.

As the meth fed on Bob, he created a safe web, almost beyond his control, and he became that zombie. One step away from being one of the stumbling, living dead of the neighborhood, but maybe that was worse.

There were still quiet nights in the house, and they could hear the fury of MOVE, but those nights were getting more distant, just as Bob seemed to be getting more distant. Two nights in a row Sharon left his room and took her chair back to the room she and Trigger used to share. After the second time, a shirtless Bob came in screaming, his hair frazzled, a half-naked wild ape. A few days later, while he was tweaked and paranoid, he nailed some wood pieces onto the frame of his bedroom door while Sharon was still in the room. Bits of the loose decking from the rear porch that he was going to rebuild and paint, but that was a lifetime ago.

Trigger stood behind him in the hall watching, while Sharon watched him watch.

"Gotta do it . . . you gotta do it . . . ," Bob mumbled to himself.

When he finished, he stood and stretched, hammer in hand, admired his work, and then went downstairs. Sharon rolled to the doorway in the bedroom, and Trigger stepped to it from the hall. He pulled on the wood to test it. Solid and resolute. She looked at him, and all he could do was look back. No, that's not exactly true. All he *did* was look back.

It was just enough so she couldn't get her chair into the hall. Captive. The bathroom had two doors, one in Bob's room and one in the hall, and she could still get through both of those, giving her access to the hallway, but Bob hadn't finished, he'd only gone downstairs to get more wood. Trigger stood behind him again as he nailed it onto the hallway jamb, this time on the bathroom door, and again Sharon watched him watch.

"Why are you doing this?" Trigger asked.

He didn't slow his frantic hammering, sweat dripping from his nose and bubbling from his massive back.

"Gotta do it . . . gotta get it done . . . ," He sputtered out a few more things that didn't make any sense. He had his reasons, as delusional and deranged as they were. He didn't want to lose what was closest to him ever again. He would keep it safely locked away where it couldn't get lost or damaged. Or leave him.

Trigger told him to stop, but Bob ignored him. Trigger yelled, then pushed on Bob's arm as he swung. Bob stopped. He stood to his full height, stretching out his shoulders like a huge condor and blocking out the hallway. His eyes were glassy and glowed red, as if they were the only exit for the fire that burned within him. He squeezed the hammer tight, lifting it up to his shoulder, seemingly beyond his control. Trigger froze, squeezing his eyes shut, panicked and unable to made a quick decision, waiting for that hammer to crush into his skull. Before it could, Sharon clapped her hands once, like calling a dog, and Bob's eyes flickered. He resumed his work, and Trigger was invisible again.

Two nights later, after both the sizzling heat of the day and the speakers at the MOVE house had quieted, and all that was left were the animals in the zoo waiting for him, Trigger crept down that dark hall on the balls of his feet, quiet and padded like a rabbit. He didn't know what drew him there. His animal instinct, he supposed. There

Bob was, his gorilla back almost entirely blocking her from view as he propped his naked body up on one forearm against hers, using his other arm to throw her dead pale legs over him, pretending she was doing it herself. As they slid off lifelessly, he would grab them with his free arm and throw them back again, like they were empty of bones, just white rubber over foam. It lit such a raging fire in Trigger; he knew right then it would never be extinguished until Bob was dead, the same way Bob must have felt when he tried to kill Trigger.

No, they reached no compromise. And the city dropped the bomb on the MOVE house, and he used the key, and the fire was lit, and they were all gonna feel the heat that summer.

# Five

When he was younger, Trigger was never exposed to religion. The only measure of right and wrong were the rules that Bob made. That was all he knew in the universe. Those rules were flexible, to say the least. There were no moral consequences, and commandments were made to fit their lifestyle, not the other way around. Animals don't have religion either. They don't have time for worrying about those rules. They have their own set of rules. Natural Law. The real law. The only law.

Natural Law was one of the beliefs the MOVE people held close. It was because of their beliefs and their actions that the city burned that night. Mayor Wilson Goode agreed to have a bomb dropped on the MOVE house, dropped from a hovering helicopter, the bomb built with military-grade explosives, and the fire allowed to burn for hours before firetrucks worked at extinguishing it. Possibly the only time in America's history when a bomb was dropped on the continental United States, and it was done by Philadelphia's own mayor.

⁂

Though the city was in a standoff with the MOVE people living in that house on Osage Avenue, the conflict had started ten years earlier.

MOVE was founded and led by John Africa; his distrust of the system began when his mother died at a young age. He blamed the hospital, where she was being treated, for her death. A high school dropout, he was drafted into the army to serve in the Korean War. Born Vincent Leaphart, he changed his name to John Africa after he returned from the war, returned to represent the continent where he claimed all life began. Africa said he had the solution to all of the problems of all of the people throughout the world and began picking up followers. They opposed science, technology, authority, and modern medicine. Although they were deeply religious, originally called the Christian Movement for Life, they were labeled radicals or anarchists or cultists or terrorists by the authorities and neighbors alike because of their strongly anti-establishment stance. Living a dualistic lifestyle, they lived in a city but aspired to return to a hunter-gatherer type of society, or what was called anarcho-primitivism, a form of noncivilized (as opposed to uncivilized) living. Re-wilding. De-evolved. They aspired to eat only raw food, nothing cooked or processed, and brought up their children—whom they saw as untainted by the system—on a completely uncooked and natural diet, even going so far as to serve them not only roots and nuts but raw chicken. They claimed respect for the lives of all animals, including the rats and insects that began to infest the neighbors' connecting rowhouses, even removing the flea collars from neighborhood pets to protect the lives of the fleas. It was said that John Africa's view of the cosmos was that it was in constant conflict, good against evil. Natural Law versus the system.

Just as the universe seemed dichotomous, so were some of MOVE's actions. They left baskets of fresh-baked breads, fruit, and vegetables out for neighbors and children to encourage healthy eating habits. They helped neighbors carry in groceries and shoveled their walks when it snowed. Yet at the same time, they would have heated exchanges with those who opposed them. They were complex, as is nature. They could build a doghouse for a neighbor or get into a violent exchange with them over a parking space. Some of the neighbors even claimed they had been physically attacked, but there was never any proof, and even if there had been, the city had shown time and time again that it was reluctant to intervene, fearing to repeat the violent confrontation of the previous decade, when MOVE had its headquarters on 33rd Street in Powelton Village, near Drexel University.

MOVE was different from Trigger. Different from everyone. Adherents were vehemently opposed to slavery of any type, and were especially enraged over the enslavement of animals. Circuses, where animals are enslaved and humiliated; puppy mills, where they are prostituted and exploited; and zoos, where they have their freedom stripped for the pleasure and profit of others.

All members of MOVE took the surname *Africa* to galvanize the fact they were family and lived by the guidelines laid out by John Africa, and to pay homage to him. Each wore their hair in dreadlocks, uncut and uncombed. Natural. They led aggressive, profane demonstrations in front of the zoo, pet stores, or any other institutional form of animal enslavement. They rallied on residential streets, clogging traffic and irritating residents who were struggling to deal with their own obstacles. Anywhere they could draw attention MOVE might be found with bullhorns, pushing their platform and getting under the city's skin. This led to constant conflict with the Philadelphia authorities and many arrests, which gave MOVE even more fuel to protest what they believed was another injustice.

During that time in Powelton Village, nearly a decade earlier, the police had claimed MOVE was causing a disturbance in the house they lived in on 33rd Street. When the police went to break up what MOVE said was a peaceful gathering, several arrests were made, leading to a scuffle that ended up with three-week-old Life Africa being knocked to the sidewalk and allegedly stepped on by an officer's boot, fatally crushing the child's skull. The MOVE organization took the case to court, but it was dismissed before all the facts could be heard. The fire was lit.

This incident drove MOVE to push back harder against the system. Neighbors began to complain to the city about the garbage around the house and the growing rat infestation problem. Some even claimed MOVE was threatening them.

The Philadelphia Police Department obtained a court order for MOVE to evacuate the house. MOVE agreed to vacate and surrender all their weapons, if the police department would release those currently incarcerated MOVE members. The police did not agree to the terms, and MOVE dug in. This led to a standoff in the house on 33rd Street where then-mayor Frank Rizzo ordered a blockade around the MOVE house, shutting off all utilities for fifty-one days and attempting to prevent any deliveries of food or water, trying to force them out.

Rizzo was the former police chief, large in stature and in personality, and he had a reputation for being hard-nosed, boisterous, and brutish. Because of his volatile relationship with Philadelphia's black community, Rizzo's critics often claimed his actions were racially motivated or unnecessarily violent and that he specifically targeted activities in black neighborhoods, so much so that residents in those neighborhoods were often reluctant to call the police for anything.

MOVE took up their arms and prepared for war. When the city's blockade tactic didn't work, Rizzo apparently became more aggressive. "They named the game, and I assure you, they lose." Rizzo promised. "The police will be in there to drag them out by the backs of their necks. They're going to be taken by force, if they resist."

A MOVE representative responded in turn. "If the police come in here with their hands, we'll use our hands. If they come in here with clubs, we'll use clubs. But if they come in here shooting and killing our women and children and our men, we will shoot back in defense of our lives."

Rizzo followed through with his promise.

At the end of the fifty-one-day siege, Rizzo rolled in fire trucks with water cannons and blasted thousands of gallons of water into the home. John Africa and his followers still refused to come out and somehow shots were fired. An officer was killed in the supposed shootout, although MOVE claimed they never even returned fire, and eyewitnesses gave accounts that the bullet had seemed to come from friendly fire. Eventually the MOVE members crawled out from the basement, some holding children in from of them, possibly to deter the police from shooting them upon their surrender. The city accused them of using the children as human shields.

One death, but it was the death of an officer.

The same day as the shootout, Rizzo instructed the house be plowed down, which it was, destroying any evidence of where the bullet could have possibly come from, along with any other evidence regarding what happened that day, erasing the incident from the public's view and the minds of most, but not all. Nine MOVE members were charged with murder. Nine were found guilty of the officer's murder. After a nineteen-week trial in which MOVE members defended themselves, frequently leading courtroom tirades against the system, all nine people were sentenced up to one hundred years each. The MOVE members were incensed, insisting that the fatal bullet had not come from within the home.

Years passed, but MOVE's position did not soften. If anything, it grew stronger and more rebellious.

After the 33rd Street shootout, the remaining MOVE members made it their mission to have their nine brothers and sisters, known as the MOVE Nine, freed from prison for a crime they insisted they had not committed, and they did this from their new home: 6221 Osage Avenue, owned by John Africa's sister, Louise James.

By constantly badgering the Osage Avenue neighborhood with protests and speakers and profanity, they hoped to gain leverage. If they could irritate the neighborhood enough, just maybe the city would have to listen to the neighbors and in turn listen to MOVE. But it didn't work out as planned. MOVE hunkered down, arming themselves, fortifying the rowhouse, and letting it be known they would respond to any aggression. When no compromise could be reached, the neighbors, unhappy with the hands-off approach of both the police and City Hall, reached out to Pennsylvania Governor Dick Thornburgh. Unwilling to lose face to the Republican administration, newly elected Democratic mayor Wilson Goode finally took action, assembling a leadership team that threw together a poorly conceived plan in just a matter of days.

⁂

On the evening of May 12, police did their best to evacuate the houses surrounding 6221 Osage Avenue and most of the adjoining neighborhood, recommending people just pack enough for an overnight stay with friends or relatives, assuring residents they would be back in their homes by the next evening, at the latest. For the most part residents left quietly; the few who argued were informed that if they stayed, they would be arrested. Any cars left on the street were towed away by the city. Then over five hundred police officers took their positions from nearby rooftops and the surrounding streets, giving them views of the front and rear of the MOVE compound, along with a clean view to their rooftop bunker. Tactical teams entered the adjacent homes that flanked the house. The rowhomes of the city were separated by thick walls, and police intended to drill through these walls and flood the home with tear gas as needed.

At 5:30 AM on the morning of Monday, May 13, 1985, a voice crackled over a bullhorn in the heavy morning air. Not the same familiar voice that constantly streamed out of the rooftop bunker speakers, but a sharp, direct, and authoritarian voice. The voice of Police Commissioner Gregore Sambor, one of the key authors of the morning's plan.

"Attention MOVE! This is America. You have to abide by the laws of the United States!" Sambor then read the list of names on his arrest warrants and continued.

"All occupants have fifteen minutes to peacefully evacuate the premises and surrender. This is your only notice. Your fifteen minutes starts now."

No response. The house lay quiet as the sun peeked over the skyline of the city, as if trying to see what was happening on Osage Avenue. Displaced neighbors woke in beds that were not their own, groggy for sleep and wondering when they would be able to return to their own homes, as MOVE and the police waited each other out.

Fifteen minutes passed, and the city awoke to a violent tempest of bullets. Over 10,000 rounds peppered the house within 90 minutes. That strange house with the bunker, and the voices, and the children in it. After the bullets failed to force them from the home, tear gas and hundreds of thousands of gallons of water doused the home, but still they refused to obey the commands and surrender.

Weary and frustrated neighbors watched from around corners, and reporters got as close as they could to the melee before the police shoved them back. Helicopters rattled over the neighborhood, catching the attention of Trigger and all the displaced families and onlookers that spilled into the street, watching a small war unfold in their neighborhood. On their street.

By 10:40 AM, the front of the home was destroyed, but the MOVE members still stood their ground and would not exit. The rooftop bunker, heavily fortified, remained in place, and the police could not seize the house, believing MOVE was heavily armed and it would be a risk to approach the house given MOVE's superior tactical position. Their first tactics had failed. Mayor Wilson Goode held a press conference stating that he intended to take the house "by any means necessary."

Around five that evening, Goode approved the use of explosives to eliminate the rooftop bunker and gain entry to the home. As the morning evaporated into a scorching afternoon and a muggy evening, the authorities of the city of Philadelphia made the irrevocable decision to bomb the house. A mixture of Tovex and C-4 (the latter provided in quantity by the FBI) was tossed from a helicopter onto the roof of the home at 5:27 PM, igniting the fire that would not only burn down the MOVE house but also sixty-one other homes, along with the souls and minds of the people of Philadelphia. The firefighters that lined the streets and flooded the house with water cannons throughout the day remained static for nearly an hour. Sambor wanted the fire to burn, in what he claimed was a tactical decision to force MOVE from the home. The bunker had not collapsed from the initial explosion, and Sambor wanted it taken out. Fire Commissioner William Richmond relayed this information to his firemen, who waited. The fire quickly raged out of control, carving a path through the plywood separators between each back porch, then moving quickly through each home while huge crowds gathered around. The heat from the flames only made the day hotter; sweat bubbled on foreheads and tickled down people's spines. Angry voices rose above the crackling fire, screaming at the authorities who had burned their entire existence to ash, all to remove thirteen people—most of whom were women and children—from one home. Others blamed MOVE for creating a war solely for their own benefit, and some were there just for the sideshow feel of it all, hopefully to be seen on a news report, yelling, throwing their hands in the air, and laughing. The national media picked it up, and the spectacle was broadcast across the country on the evening news.

By the next morning, the inferno had obliterated all sixty-one burned homes and had killed eleven of the people in the MOVE house, including five children, the group's leader John Africa, and a teenager named Tree Africa, the teenage girl Trigger's age. Two survivors managed to clamor out of the flames, eyes stinging. They were burnt, saturated, and exhausted. Ramona Africa and thirteen-year-old Birdie Africa.

The ash snowed down over the neighborhood and the animals in the Philadelphia Zoo.

Immediately after the incident, it was revealed that just two days before the bombing, MOVE had sent a threatening letter to neighbors, the neighbors they had once baked bread for. It seemed they realized a final showdown was imminent, and they were playing every card they had, again leaning on the neighbors to gain leverage and control their fate.

"If MOVE go down, not only will everyone in this block go down, the knee joints of America will break, and the body of America will soon fall. Before we let you muthafuckers make an example of us, we will burn this muthafucking house down and burn you all up with us."

In light of this letter, Commissioner Sambor stated that it was his "personal opinion" that MOVE "started or assisted" the fire, possibly by saturating the roofs with gasoline. Mayor Goode suggested that MOVE was "a group that was bent on absolute destruction, a group that was, in fact, a guerrilla group inside an urban area." The duality of the cosmos. The theory that MOVE had saturated the roofs with gas, in an ultimate act of defiance to go down as martyrs and to infect a generation, could never be verified, and it seemed just another strange anomaly in a strange string of events that culminated with the fire that ravaged and gutted a neighborhood of families caught in the middle of a war.

♣

Trigger hid in the zoo that night, where the animals had their own issues.

After the bombing, most nights he would find himself standing in front of the rubble of the MOVE home, staring into the charred remains and still feeling the heat of their convictions. A full square block of the city, burnt to the ground.

The whole neighborhood smelled of wet smoke and century-old lumber, the homes crumpled into piles of memories with just the brick firewalls left standing between. He wondered if they had removed the bodies, the bones left in the embers, and if he was breathing in the ashes of the dead. Tree Africa, his age, was now frozen in time, like the rest of them, their lost spirits trapped, drifting forever in the ashy river of the streets, seemingly pulled in a direction beyond their control and not knowing enough to care anyway.

♣

There was only so much time he could spend wandering between the zoo and the ghosts of Osage Avenue. It was almost four miles between the two, and both vied for his full attention, dragging him back and forth between his two obsessions. Wearing down his still developing body and mind. But at some point, he had to go to the house to take a shower and wash off the stink of the city. If he was lucky, Bob would be in the basement.

When the fire burned down those sixty-one homes, the filthy home lab that supplied much of the area with meth, that used to supply Bob with his meth, burned down too. Brazen, industrious young men saw the void as an opportunity to push their new product, crack cocaine, but Big Bob was already established in his basement and he quickly moved to fill the void in the meth market. But there wasn't enough room for all of them to profit without conflict.

There was a reason he was called Big Bob, at least there used to be. He stood six-foot-four and was broad and thick across the shoulders and chest, with a dense square jaw. When he was younger, he had played middle linebacker for Upper Darby High School, one of the biggest schools in Philadelphia. He was so big and aggressive that he was the starting middle linebacker for the varsity team when just a freshman. He made All-State twice and got a full ride to a few schools but never went to college. He got a girl pregnant in his senior year and had to forgo college to get a job and support his baby and new wife. Not too long after, the new wife fled with the new baby, leaving him with only the broken memories of the destiny he'd lost.

He recovered though, falling deeply in love again, this time with Trigger's mother. He was happy and content, ready to live out the rest of his life with her and their love, but the universe does what it wants and doesn't care what our plans are. After she died in the car crash, it was too much for him to deal with, losing everything twice. That was when he needed an escape, and he had been escaping ever since, deciding to live by his guidelines alone. Respected once, now he was shriveled. Still tall but dried out, shrinking and circling the dead like a vulture. The name Big Bob was now bigger than the man. A once proud, productive member of society, he had withered away over time because of loss and what he believed was an inescapable fate, an unfair fate. So Big Bob slowly changed to just Bob, and Trigger hated this version of him. Trigger hated his frazzled hair, like he had been struck by lightning in a cartoon, and his meth-brown teeth. His faced pocked and scabbed, with bleeding scratch marks on his neck and the back of his furry-knuckled hands. He hated Bob's hairy, shirtless chest with that long silver chain, the key tangled in that curly gray nest between his nipples. He was ape-like in every way, and Trigger wanted to hurt him. No longer a man, no longer contributing to the good of humanity in any way. He lived for himself alone. A disconnected and solitary animal, hiding from the world in this disintegrating cave of a house. He took what he wanted, and his dreams were the dreams of the dead.

Trigger's dreams were the dreams the animals had.

❧

Not long after the bombing, school let out, and Smiley had promised Trigger a present for passing, and proof of it. Trigger brought Smiley his report card during their lunch break. He was the only one who had asked to see it. His grades were good, and Smiley was pleased. The present was a hamster, Smiley's own pet he said he couldn't keep any longer. He had brought the small wire cage, full of wood chips and fluff, and food for it to eat, and it sat on the picnic bench waiting for Trigger before he even got there, even before Smiley had seen Trigger's report card.

Smiley had fifteen employees under him, but he almost always made time to have lunch with Trigger, who usually brought his lunch with him after buying a sandwich at the corner store. There was almost never food at the house now, and if something *did* happen to show up, the dead would swarm from the basement or the front stoop. If he could get to it fast enough, though, he would take all he could grab and bring it up to Sharon.

"Here he is!" Smiley said, with that wide grin. He reached his waxy long fingers into the cage and pulled the hamster out gently, explaining how he was giving it to Trigger to care for, then holding it to his lips and whispering something to it, but Trigger couldn't make out what. Smiley placed it into Trigger's cupped hands. He could feel its tiny, soft feet splayed out, its body trembling with quick shallow breaths. He closed his hands around it and stroked its back with his finger.

"That's right," Smiley said. "An animal is only as good as its handler. Dog don't bite you 'cause it's mean, dog bites you 'cause it's scared. Scared of what it don't know. It only knows what it's been taught."

Trigger wanted to hold that hamster for the rest of his life. Protect it. Give it a family. It would always have someone looking out for it, and he would always have something waiting for him, wanting to see him.

After work he carried the cage back to the house and thought deeply about the hamster. Its place in that cage and in his world. He decided to give the hamster to Sharon. Something for her to care for. Something to force her to have a purpose. It was a risk, with Bob in there, but he convinced himself that the risk was worth what Sharon could gain. What he could gain by helping her.

The front door was cracked, which he was used to seeing. He made his way up the spalling concrete steps and across the porch, solid and aged, stopping at the top step for just a moment, as if he had forgotten something. He spun around, and there across the street was the woman with the cat eyeglasses. She sat on a folding chair on her porch. She had watched him coming down the street. She waved a thin, spotted hand. He turned his head, pretending not to see, and stepped inside.

Directly inside was the small living room with the brown couch and cluttered coffee table. Past the couch and to the right, just before the kitchen, were the stairs leading up to the second floor, and beneath those stairs was the door to the basement. The floors throughout were brown hardwood, and immediately inside, the light dulled and the entire interior of the home felt like a musty cavern. There was an instant dimming, as if the doorway were the threshold between day and night. Dark and light. The last bulbs were burning out. The house was one step ahead of sunset, darkening just before the last bit of daylight subsided. But it always seemed dark to him. Muffled music came from the basement, and the dank living room was empty except for the trash and bottles on the coffee table and around the couch. He stopped a second and stared, looking first at the hamster, then across the room. Maybe it was a mistake. Empty cigarette packs, a bowl of ash and butts. Matches and chip bags, beer bottles and soda cans. It needed to be cleaned up, but Trigger just didn't feel like he should be the one to do it.

Upstairs he saw right into Sharon's bedroom, Bob's bedroom. She was in her wheelchair in front of the dresser, looking out the rear window, a wisp of smoke twisting above her head in the stifling heat. Just a dresser and bed in the room, leaving space for her to navigate around any clothes on the floor. She stared out the window into the rear yard. There wasn't much to look at out there, just the other brick rowhouses and the concrete pad of a backyard. Sprigs of long weeds peeked their way through the cracks in the concrete, fighting for life in that barren yard in West Philadelphia. Above them were the backs of the other homes, and windows of other houses, with other people in them looking out toward something they thought might be better.

Sharon heard him come in and tried to hide the pipe beneath a book on the dresser, then spun the chair around to see him. Her hair was long and smooth, a dry brown, the hair of an older lady, and her eyes were the same, brown marbles on the crumpled white sheet of her scabbed face, distant like they had been through a war, like she was in a war.

The room was the only space in the house somewhat organized and uncluttered, but that's not to say it was clean. No rooms in the house were actually clean, even Trigger's room. They were dark, lit—if at all—by faded old light bulbs in lamps with no shades. Tight, and closing in.

He placed the cage on the bed and took the hamster out, letting it feel its way over the sheets. New smells and places. She picked it up with her thin fingers and stared right into its eyes, locked into it, then rubbed its fur against her chafed lips and whispered to it, just as Smiley had done.

"It's from Smiley," he said.

He spoke to her a bit about Smiley, the kind of man he was and how Smiley treated him. Trigger was proud, and Sharon saw that in him.

"He sounds like a good person," she said, still looking into the hamster's eyes.

It hurt to give it to her, but he didn't let on. He felt guilt twist in his stomach for putting it in the room with Bob when the only person it had ever known was Smiley, but he wanted Sharon to have it, maybe for his own selfish reasons. If she somehow felt better, then maybe he would too.

Trigger went to wash his face in the bathroom, and he saw her round wheel of pills on the sink, right next to his toothpaste, a few punched out of the plastic. He rubbed it between his fingertips and looked into the water-spotted mirror. The image of Bob's hairy back laying on top of her, doing what he wanted with her, flooded back into his mind, and how she was trapped, and how he himself was the one who trapped her there. It was better than the alternative he figured, but how he hated Bob.

What did they whisper?

He put the pills down and went to lie on the mattress that lay flat on the floor of his room. The voices in the basement began to rise with the moon, and it seemed like a good night to get to the zoo. But he had to lie down for just a little, it was so warm and he was so tired. Always so tired. Sleep took him on the bare mattress.

He woke up damp with sweat to the blaring music, now out of the basement and in the living room. Stuffing some things in his backpack, he went to slip out. In the hallway, his bony body leaning against the stair banister in front of the bathroom, was one of the dead. It was an image frozen with clarity, one that would arise now and then, beyond his control. Gangly, with greasy black hair and a thin black goatee painted on his chalky skin. His eyes were red slits. Relaxed, high, and smiling, he leered into the bathroom, like a bratty kid at the zoo teasing an animal.

When Trigger went to slide past that shady figure in the hall, he saw Sharon in the bathroom, on the toilet, with the chair beside her, no door on the bathroom and exposed to the world. The man stood in the hallway, scarcely a man, a living corpse, just staring at her, and she was just staring at the floor, scratching feverishly at her forearm so hard she drew blood. Even at Trigger's young age he had dealt with the dead plenty of times before, but his way of dealing with them was mostly just to ignore them, like the rest of society did, like most people do when they see something that makes them uncomfortable. Most people don't want to believe that what is in those people is in all of us, that we are all the same type of animal.

This time, he felt something different. He had to look at it. He had to deal with it. His frail chest puffed out some and blood pumped into his arms. He stepped into the bathroom and found a towel, and with his back to Sharon, held it draped in the door opening.

A thin voice croaked behind the towel, that burned out, lazy drawl that the dead spoke with.

"Come on little man . . . don't keep it all to yourself."

A gray crabbed hand pulled the towel to the side to peep in.

"Get the fuck out!" Trigger yelled, and kicked under the towel, hitting nothing. The head disappeared and he could be heard shambling back downstairs, giggling.

Trigger stared into that towel and clinched his eyes tight, forcing the tears back into his head.

When the toilet flushed and he knew she was out, he dropped the towel right there and went into the hall to leave, but she called him in as he passed the bedroom door.

"Come here," she said, her voice drifting across the bedroom into the hall.

"See, he likes it here." She held the hamster in her palm and stroked its back with the knuckles on her frail fingers, rubbing the soft fur on the scabs of her hand.

"How can anyone like it here?" he said, trembling with anger. "We can't live like this . . ."

She held her corpse finger to her dry lips to silence him. "Shhhh, everything will be fine," she said, placing the hamster back in its cage and locking the hasp. She put the cage on the table by the window, letting the fading light of the day spill through the thin wire bars.

"You like the animals," she said, staring into the cage. "I guess you get to see all them animals at the zoo." She rattled her fingernail lightly against the bars of the cage like she was strumming a harp. "I like animals too. Maybe someday you can help them out, like being a vet or something. That would be nice. It's something I would do."

"Maybe you should then, get some kind of vet education . . ."

"No," she said, "it's too late for me. I didn't even graduate high school or nothing."

"Too late? Your seventeen."

"I got no education, I can't do nothing like that. No diploma. No prom."

He looked at the cold chrome on the chair, and her in it, and the gloominess of the room and her universe, and he felt the weight of it on his thin shoulders, making him slouch forward. He didn't want to see it. He wanted to see her get up and run down the stairs, laughing, into the street, where she could spin in circles with her arms out, soaking in the sunlight. He wanted to spin with her, the two of them careless and light as blown soap bubbles carried on the summer air. Free to move and laugh and dream of things they dared not dream now.

She spun her chair beside the bed and pulled herself out, rolling her body face up and staring into the ceiling, the same ceiling she always stared at. The same thoughts she always thought. When her reality became too much, and she felt as if that faded ceiling were pressing in on her, as if the walls were squeezing her in, she imagined that ceiling were the endless universe and she could go anywhere she wanted, with a body light and healthy and strong. And if she couldn't imagine it, if she couldn't have it, she would smother out the entire universe so no one could. He watched her drift away from him as she lay on the bed, and he would rather her drift away than have her there, knowing she knew he was the one that put her there.

He left and started down the stairs, pausing to look at the room of dead, prone beneath a haze of smoke on the brown couch. When he went to adjust his backpack, he realized he wasn't even wearing it; the smoke was getting to him too. He hopped back up the stairs to get it, and from the corner of his eye saw the lighter flicker in Sharon's room. She left the only way she could, while he left through the front door.

# Six

THE FIRST FEW NIGHTS HE SLEPT AT THE ZOO, he was scared. Not scared of the animals, or even getting caught; he didn't even really know what he was afraid of. It was just him and the moonlight and the grunting of animals talking about the new creature. The new prisoner.

The master key would get him in, but a guard usually wandered around the 34th Street entrance or the service doors on Zoological Drive. It was a risk to use a door, so he clipped a small section of tension wire and some tie wires on the bottom of the chain-link fence on Zoological Drive, near the wolf exhibit, so he could squeeze his frail body under it. There was a decent patch of trees and shrubs along the fence line, all around the rear of the zoo, that would provide cover. He could easily sleep there, next to some barrels and fiberglass rocks that were stacked up next to the exhibit, away from where visitors would see them, but there were much better places to go. Places he liked to walk past in the daylight when he was working. The bird sanctuary, the African plains, the prairie dog exhibit. He just had to avoid the guards to get to them.

This night was so hot he just sat in the brush, beside the wolf exhibit, soaking up the steam from the earth, alone with his thoughts like Sharon was alone with hers. He was selfish and a coward and had left her to survive with her own problems, in her own zoo. His mind worked through uncomfortable thoughts, filling uncomfortable, empty time.

The heat drove him to water, like it does to all animals. Even when they know there's danger, but the thirst is so powerful the body overrules the mind. He needed to head toward the snack shack, the closest building to the wolf habitat and, he figured, the safest. The only problem was there was no shortcut through the exhibits. He could usually move through the zoo without going on the walking paths at all by cutting through exhibits, depending on where he wanted to be, but not if he wanted to get to the snack shack. For that, he had to use the paths where the night security guards typically patrolled, observing nearly everything. Two of them, separately walking miles each night around the zoo, looking for any issues with the animals or anything out of the ordinary.

He became a ghost, invisible and unknown.

From where Trigger was, there was no safe way to the shack, he just had to run for it as quietly, as invisibly, as he could. It was probably under a minute, but it felt like every step he took was as loud as thunder. Once he got there, he couldn't stay long because the guards would go in and steal stuff too, so he loaded up his backpack with a few sodas, chips, pretzels and peanuts, and a candy bar. Breakfast and a few snacks for the next day.

From there he could easily get to the bird sanctuary without stepping on the concrete paths, cutting across a picnic area and a small wooded plot to get to it. That was his favorite. Since he was working the next day, he could stay there and not worry for the night. Nobody ever went in, and he was free, living in the jungle. De-evolved. He heard the birds and watched them hop from tree limb to tree limb. They were free in their own minds, and he felt free in there with them. It was like they didn't know they were enclosed, and it made him feel like maybe he could feel that way too, somehow, in that sanctuary. It was green and moist and quiet, and no other beings in the universe except for the birds knew he was there. There was a small waterfall and plants with thick green leaves that scraped against a little wooden bridge. That's where he went, under that bridge. The birds squawked and shouted out to each other about him, and he just laid back and listened. Re-wilding. He could close his eyes and be somewhere else, give his mind a rest from its relentless conflicts. He listened to the high chatter of the birds and the sound of the water riffling away like his thoughts, and it helped him forget that he was under an artificial bridge inside a giant cage in the Philadelphia Zoo.

⁂

Rabbit rabbit.

He always slept light, never fully resting, ready to jump up and go, and the first rays of the morning woke him. He heard the birds and the water, they were in his dreams all night, and for a few seconds he totally forgot where he was, who he was. Just a random animal waking up in the jungle. A few seconds of nothingness, and it was the best feeling he could have. Probably how Sharon felt when she got high. No memory of an unwanted past, no future to fret over.

Smiley said if you say *rabbit rabbit* first thing in the morning on the first day of a new month, you'll have good luck all that month. Good things will happen to you. Trigger said it every morning just to increase his odds, figuring it couldn't hurt, since he needed all the good luck he could get.

He ate the peanuts under the bridge and saved the candy bar for later, something to look forward to. There was a bathroom outside of the bird sanctuary, and he crept to it, taking his gray zoo shirt out of his backpack and changing into it. He started keeping a toothbrush, toothpaste, and a washrag in his backpack, not knowing for sure when he would be sleeping in a bed or amongst the animals. Washing his face with just water, he checked his fortitude in the mirror and prepared for another day.

After leaving the bathroom, he waited in the cover provided by a patch of brush and watched the service entry gate on Zoological Drive as the workers started coming in. After Smiley and few others entered, he slipped out from his hiding place and blended into the flow, walking freely down the concrete trail and on into the maintenance building.

Smiley put him on trash duty. Trash duty basically meant wandering the zoo and picking up any trash on the grounds and emptying any full cans, but what it meant to him was freedom, as it also gave him more time alone. He always thought Smiley gave him trash duty because he knew how much he liked it. Trigger was only part-time and the youngest on the crew by far, and trash duty was the easiest job, so someone like him wouldn't normally get the assignment. But Smiley gave it to him, and when he did, Trigger, all day, was alone, with his thoughts.

He could roam the zoo, watching the animals and the people, all while getting his $3.35 an hour. The paths were wide and snaked around the entire zoo, connecting with each other so people could easily see everything without much backtracking. Each path would always lead him in a familiar direction, and he pretended they were streets in a comfortable neighborhood where he lived. He saw the animals that shared a home with him at night and smiled to himself about the secret they kept together. If he wanted to watch the big cats sprawled in the sun, he could. He could watch them roll and roar, and maybe they seemed content for a while, and maybe that meant he could be content at some point too. And if they wanted to go back inside to spend the afternoon alone with their thoughts, they could do that too, and so could he. He reasoned they were not that different. Not just him and the cats, but him and all of the animals, and he felt it gave him a place where he belonged.

He sometimes followed young families with their children, just out of their view, and he could daydream he was one of them as well. He trailed them as they walked, lagging behind just enough to hear what they were saying and pretending they were speaking to him, and he was so comfortable with them that he didn't have to answer. All the while scanning the grounds for litter. Taking pride in keeping his zoo clean. He stretched into corners and behind shrubs and scraped up gum and ice cream cones covered with ants. Spotless and organized and everything as it should be.

At lunch outside the maintenance shed, Smiley leaned his chair back against the white concrete building, balancing on two chair legs, his bony shoulders pinned against the wall, smiling in thought at a few white clouds.

"You ever see a palm tree?" he asked.

"No."

"In San Diego, you look up, see those big palm leaves against the blue sky, it's like you died and gone to heaven, man." He took a bite of apple and squinted an eye into the core. "Some people say they got the best zoo there too, in San Diego. But the best zoo in the country is right here. Right in Philly. First zoo too. You know that?"

"Yeah, I know. It's the first zoo." There were signs and plaques all around the zoo commemorating its rich history.

"Damn right."

Trigger crunched a pretzel and read the back of the bag.

"Smiley, how do you get a GED?"

Smiley looked down from the clouds and his face flattened out. He dropped the chair forward onto all four legs and pointed a gnarled finger at Trigger's face, bending it around the apple.

"You dropping out of school? Don't let me hear you say it, son." His eyes got narrow and the deep smile lines were just as wrinkled, only with a frown.

"No, not me. I was just wondering."

Smiley tilted his head and squinted harder, then nodded and that huge smile was back. "Good, cause your Uncle Sam don't wanna hear that shit. Got enough dumb ass niggers running around here, don't need another one. You stay in school. Learn something." He took another bite of his apple and, holding it in his hand, with his free index finger began plucking at the long fingers on his other hand, one at a time with each point he made.

"You young . . . you white . . . you got a job . . . you smart. You way ahead of the game. Plus," he dragged the back of his sleeve across his mouth, "you got a great uncle!" He threw his head back and laughed out loud. For him it was just a small chuckle, but to Trigger it was a sound that boomed like a cannon across all of West Philadelphia.

"It ain't for me," Trigger said again. "I was just wondering."

"Good, 'cause I seen plenty of people 'round here using these streets as an excuse, and that's just what it is. An excuse. I guess," he continued, "if you need, you can find something like that at the li-berry."

He tipped his chair back again, shutting his eyes and letting the sun beat on his face, dark skin soaking in the rays.

"Know what else they got out there besides palm trees and the second-best zoo? Beaches. Blue water. Not no brown water like down the shore. Out there it's all blue."

He sat there with his eyes closed, enjoying the images of San Diego's palm trees and blue water, as Trigger took the last swig of his soda and got up to stretch his back.

Without opening his eyes, he said, "And my boy."

Trigger knew Smiley had a son, but he never really spoke about him.

"Yeah, he living it up out there with his momma. Boy is just about your age, thirteen, fourteen or so, right?"

Trigger didn't respond and Smiley didn't continue. He just sat there with that wide smile spread across his face, imagining San Diego.

Later that day, as the sun began to drop and the temperature tweaked down slightly from sweltering to merely smothering, Trigger started his unconscious pilgrimage back to the MOVE house. His heavy legs moved by instinct as his mind worked to stave off the loneliness. Some streets were dark and quiet, some were lit with streetlamps and alive with people and sounds and smells. People shouting out to neighbors or sitting on the front stoop to get out of their hot brick houses, talking about their day or their anger about what had happened down the street. But he was just a witness. Never contributing. Colorless among the animation, almost translucent. Invisible. He just kept drifting. Thinking and drifting, both beyond his control, and then he would arrive. Staring into the ash and bones of the buildings, rows of them, like a burned-out civilization that time has moved on from but which still reaches out for remembrance.

But MOVE had time on its side, and what looked to be forgotten had just planted seeds.

They called it *The Duration of the Struggle.*

They accepted the fact that the fruits of their labor, their vision, might not be harvested by them, or their children, or their children's children. Whether their convictions, their *Guidelines*, were right, wrong, or misunderstood in the eyes of others, at the least they wanted to be the first to start the wheels turning, to create the change they believed necessary. A revolution against the perceived system. De-evolution.

Just by chance, the middle of the street divided life and death, the wind happening to blow in one direction that day and not another, and so sparing some at the cost of another row on the other side of the block. Trigger sat on a step across the street imagining the screaming ghosts of the very recent past, the backs of his legs and palms cooled by the concrete, staring into the burned-out remains.

"Hey, Nee-Gro! Whatchu doing out here, boy?"

On the corner toward the end of the street, a black kid with a red Phillies hat on backward yelled out. He and another kid jogged across the abandoned intersection toward Trigger. It was the Thomas brothers, Will and Troy. Two kids that Trigger tried his best to avoid. They weren't really brothers, they just had the same last name and were constantly together. Will was a year older than Trigger, and Troy two, but they were all in the same grade. Trigger stood and began calmly walking away, not running. Smiley always said an animal that runs from its predator sparks the instinct to kill.

Will was the one who had beaten him up at the zoo when Trigger tried to get him to stop harassing the animals. He was also the one who first called him Nigger, and Nee-Gro, and he did his best to keep the name alive and take credit for it whenever he could. He was smaller than Trigger, tight cropped hair always under that backwards wide-brimmed hat. He had a thick, ugly scar that ran from his right ear almost to his chin. He'd had it for as long as Trigger had known him, and it wasn't from an accident. When Will was younger, his father had cracked a beer bottle across Will's face when he thought the boy had talked to the police about him, which he didn't even do, and he wouldn't ever even think of doing after that. He was tight with muscles like a panther and as black and irritated as one, double-dipped and dark as Smiley. Troy was bigger, taller, and heavier. He was light-skinned, and some older kids called him high yellow, or banana. His face was round and smooth, and he had a perfectly round afro puffed out four inches above his head. They were both members of a local street gang, and this area was where they worked, selling on the corners to the drugged and dead. The gang's older members wore trench coats and derbies, like they were from the 1920s, but Will and Troy were young and still working their way through the ranks. They hated Trigger, especially Will. Troy hated him just because it was the thing to do to prove how hard he was, but Will had a different kind of hatred, a venom few have even after a lifetime of disappointment. Trigger could see it in his small black eyes, piercing, almost as if there were a fire reflecting in there when he looked at him. From the first day they'd met, Will was on him, and he'd gotten Troy on him too. They'd beaten the shit out of him so many times he could tell the difference between Will's stinging bony fists and Troy's hammering ones.

More than the beatings themselves, it was the humiliation of taking them in front of everyone at school. He was one of only a few white kids and the only one in their class. He was different. Straight blonde hair and light blue eyes. Freckles and pale skin, like he had never seen the sun. He couldn't be any more opposite, a white dot pushed around in a sea of black. They had Adidas sneakers, and Eagles and Sixers jerseys. He had canvas sneakers and whatever dirty shirt he could find lying around. They had bowls of cereal for breakfast, and peanut butter and jelly for lunch. He got by on whatever he could scavenge from the house, that he could make, or that he bought at the corner store. Not only was he the only white kid, he was the poorest and filthiest kid as well. Trigger would never even have a chance to earn any dignity, let alone keep it, as long as they were in his world.

He didn't make it more than half a block before they caught up to him.

Will had a way of walking by and knocking his shoulder into Trigger's, testing him and saying, "You wanna give it a go?" He did it constantly and almost always where plenty of people were around to see Trigger silently shrink up. Sometimes Will would slap him in the back of the head or dance around throwing jabs just inches from his face. The more people around, the more aggressive Will was, the more of a show he would put on, and the more Trigger had to tolerate it.

Will grabbed his arm and spun him around. Trigger stood there with his head down, never making eye contact.

"Where you going Nee-Gro? We hear Big Bob doing some cooking. That right? Big Bob cooking up in yo house?"

Trigger raised his shoulders in question, keeping his eyes on the cracked sidewalk. If he looked up at Will, then Will might take it as a challenge, though if he kept looking at the street, he might get sucker-punched. It was a no-win. Meanwhile, the heat rose from the ashes across the street.

Will slapped Trigger's face, just enough to let him know he wanted his attention, not enough to hurt him. A car rolled past, slowing at the MOVE house. Trigger could see the black faces inside, first looking at the remains of the home, then at him and the Thomas brothers crowding in. Trigger stared into those faces. Someone seeing and maybe doing the right thing. Pulling over to help another person out, to do what was right. The head in the passenger's seat nodded, and the car drove off, taking any hope with it.

"You know whose territory this is, don't you?" Troy asked. His voice wasn't angry, it was calm and flat.

Trigger bobbed his head and whispered yes, so softly only the spirits on the street could hear.

"Don't you?" Troy asked again.

Again Trigger said yes, this time loud enough for them to hear, looking up to make sure they heard.

"Good. You make sure everybody in that crack house of yours know that too. Cause if our people catch your people working out here . . ." Troy pulled his T-shirt up just enough to show the butt of a gun wedged in between his jeans and his soft brown stomach. There were rumors that he'd killed someone when he was fourteen, Trigger's age. It may have been just a rumor, a rumor started by Troy himself most likely, but Trigger believed it. It made him think about maybe bribing Troy to shoot Bob, not that he had anything to bribe him with.

Troy pulled his shirt down and Will grabbed Trigger by the scruff of the neck and held his face close, his eyes drilling. Trigger hunched his shoulders and held his breath. Will pushed him back and Troy turned to leave, but Will kept staring.

"How's that sweet sister of yo's doing? Maybe she'll give me a go . . ." He threw his hands above his shoulders and smiled, ducking his head and doing some kind of bouncing dance to music only he could hear. "If Big Bob's through fucking her, right?"

"Let's go." Troy called without looking back.

Will spun away, dancing down the burnt-out street and fading into the shadows of the moonlight, like a demon prancing through a graveyard.

# Seven

BY THE MIDDLE OF SUMMER, THE CLEANUP OF Osage Avenue was grinding on, clearing the debris and memories from history, the system scraping away the MOVE ideals and hoping the scorched earth would never let their seeds sprout again. Teams of city workers with backhoes and dump trucks knocked down any charred black framing left standing on the homes, dropping it into the ash that billowed into the air. Residents who had lost everything watched from a safe distance, hoping beyond hope that something would be found in the scorched remains of their lives and returned to them. A handful of homes on the outer edge of the fire weren't totally destroyed, and some memories were held intact. If the owner didn't get to them fast enough though, they would be gone. Soon after the fire, the dead of the streets rose and picked through anything of value, scavenging the memories of residents who had worked so hard to get there.

With the removal of debris, the clouds of dust and ash rose each day, not as thick as the smoke on the Monday after Mother's Day but just as painful to watch. Each ash flake reminded the displaced neighbors that everything they had and had worked for was gone, and they would be forced to start over.

Eventually only the teetering brick firewalls remained, with a bed of ash and rubble beneath piled in the center of each home's ghost. Over time everything would be leveled and swept clean. The homeowners who had lost everything would eventually be offered new homes on the same plots of land, provided by the city. They were built fast, to try and put bandages over the exposed wounds, but they were shabbily built. The roofs leaked. There were structural issues. The values of the new homes would turn to near nothing over time. This would lead to another ongoing battle between the weary residents of Osage Avenue and the city, one that would take decades to rectify.

*The Duration of the Struggle.*

❧

Trigger was able to get a study guide for the GED test and smuggled it to Sharon. He even tried to help her study, but her still-undiagnosed dyslexia made it difficult to comprehend things, and Trigger didn't understand why she didn't understand. Besides that, the subjects in the guide were beyond his knowledge, and she had little education, so it seemed futile.

Bob was spending even more time in the basement. Traffic in the house increased, and so did Bob's share of the neighborhood's business. People began to notice. Although crack was the new, profitable drug, there were still plenty of the street dead who wanted their meth. Sometimes the smell would make its way upstairs and even into the street out front, drawing them in like ants to a sweet trap.

The more meth Bob made, the more of the street dead roamed the house, and the angrier he seemed to get, even though it was what he wanted. Creating an army of near-dead, while slowly dying himself. And if he was making money, none of it went into that house or his lifestyle. They were as close to homeless as you could get while still living under a roof.

Once Trigger stayed six nights straight at the zoo, which was the most he had ever done. Smiley saw him early in the morning twice, both before almost anyone else was in, and both on days he wasn't working. He figured he had to stay clear for a little, that Smiley might begin to wonder.

Before he had clipped the fence and made his nest at the zoo, he'd spent a lot of nights just wandering the streets, just waiting until he was tired enough to go home and pass out in his room, but that was too dangerous. He could have gotten beaten up or robbed, or worse. Not that he had anything of value (other than the little money hidden in the strap of his backpack), but people sometimes don't even really want anything, they just want you to know that some shitty little piece of blacktop is their area and that they'll defend it against all comers. Territorial behavior. It's common in the animal kingdom.

After Smiley saw him, he tried to stay at the house for a few nights, spending his days picking through the remnants of MOVE, not even knowing what he was looking for. He stirred up their spirits, and they swirled around him like ashy gray ghosts. Though he couldn't say why, he felt there was something he was compelled to find. Something he needed to make sense of, and he scraped away at the clutter, searching. It wasn't an object. It was an idea, the same idea he believed in. It was nothing he could ever hold, but he still felt like there was something there and he didn't know how else to look for it. He pulled away scrap iron and tangled wire beneath the ash. His hands were sore, and the sweat dripped from his shaggy hair and off the tip of his nose. He found nothing but dirt and brick and charred wood, and more questions about why this had happened, and how, if he held the same ideas about freedom, he could prevent it from happening in his life.

At night, back at home, he would lay on his mattress and sweat, hearing the footsteps creaking up the stairs, then the grunting and the bed groaning beneath Bob's weight, but he never heard Sharon. He imagined her dead legs thrown around and that hairy back, and the images came to his mind uncontrolled. After a few minutes it would stop, then he would hear the steps again strain as Bob made his way back to his cave.

❧

Rabbit rabbit.

One morning he woke with the sun pouring into his room through the shadeless window, as if he were under a heat lamp in a glass tank, and he was surprised that he'd slept through the night.

He stuffed his backpack again with some clothes and a small towel, then went to check on Sharon before creeping out, but Bob was still in there. Their eyes met, and Bob stood, lumbering across the room. It was morning, and he wasn't high yet, and still at his full size. He had the paperback GED study guide rolled in his hand.

"Where'd this come from?" pointing it in Trigger's face, then smacking it into his open fist.

Sharon was in a light, shear nightgown, the same one she always wore, sitting in her chair. Her eyes were red and puffy, and she was pinching at her nose. A few drops of blood had trickled onto the delicate but dirty lace of the nightgown.

"You bringing this shit in here? Filling her head with crap?" He flung the study guide at Trigger, and it dropped to the worn hardwood.

"You better get your head right. And what's this?" He tromped past Sharon to the hamster cage, shoving his thick hand through the thin wire door and pulling it out.

Helpless in his fist, only its tiny head exposed, whiskers twitching feverishly.

"Rats? You bringing rats into this house? Did I say you could do that?"

That fist hung out, fresh gashes and black scabs, close to Trigger's face, squeezing the hamster tight. Trigger could imagine the pressure and could see the helpless creature's eyes water, as if all the liquid in its body were being forced into its head, nose quivering and those watery eyes looking right into his.

"Don't!" Trigger balled up his scrawny little fist as best he could and swung at Bob, clipping him in the neck. Bob brushed it off and backhanded his knuckles into Trigger's left eye, hamster, fist, and face all mashing together for an instant.

"Nothing changes," Bob said. "She don't change. You want to leave, then leave. Go live in that zoo with all the other animals for all I care. Better for me." He tilted his head and furrowed his shaggy eyebrows. "Yeah, you don't think I know? Go live there, but she stays right here. Right here with me."

The pressure of Bob's grip was crushing both the hamster's bones and Trigger's spirit, and just as Trigger thought Bob was going to squeeze the life out of both of them, a thin white hand reached up, small fingernails with no polish and chewed ragged to the skin. Sharon laid it on Bob's arm, and the rage in his eyes dialed back. He looked at her, and she looked back at him as if she were the only thing in the world that understood his rage. No. That's not exactly true. She looked at him like she *was* his world and he was hers, and she had no choice in it because of Trigger. Like she and Bob were in some minor war together that no one else could see or ever understand, and she told Bob just with that look that he could relax, and he did. His grip loosened, and the hamster could breathe again. Trigger could breathe again. His arm dropped, and she held out her hand, and he placed it into her small, soft palm. Without a word, she had tamed that wild gorilla.

Bob went to leave the room, but passing Trigger he couldn't resist the urge to again claim dominance, so he pushed Trigger up against the wall, twisting his shirt with his fist. He got really close, his pocked nose almost touching Trigger's, brown mouth breathing its stink on him, into him. Death. A fourteen-year-old kid trying to stare down his dad, and he didn't have it in him. Trigger's chin started to quiver, and he thought for sure he was going to just collapse into a puddle of tears.

"She's never leaving me. You . . . you're on your own."

Bob stomped down the steps and left, not bothering to shut the front door behind him. It was quiet, for once, and they were the only two in the house.

Trigger held off until he was gone, then slumped to the floor and cried. Sharon wheeled back to her window and looked out.

"We can't do this," he said, clearing his face with the back of his hand. "We gotta get out of here."

"How? Go where?" she asked, still looking out of the fogged glass. "Do what?"

"I don't know. I'll kill him if I have to."

"Then what do you think will happen, Trey?"

He hadn't thought that far ahead, just like when he stole the key to the zoo. He just wanted Bob gone.

"Here's what'll happen," she said, answering her own question. "You'll go in the foster system or they'll try you as an adult, and I'll probably go to some state hospital program for people like me. Poor people like me. We don't know anyone. We don't have no one else to help us. Nobody is gonna help us. You see what they did down the street, on Osage Avenue, when those people asked for help? They burned the whole block down."

He stopped crying and dragged the back of his wrists across his face to dry the tears. Exhausted, he sat there drained. "It's gotta be better than this."

"Why? Why does it gotta be better? Who says it won't be worse? I don't know what's out there, neither do you. At least here we know. It's not good, but we know what it is."

"Maybe when you turn eighteen you can adopt me, so I don't go into foster care, and we can live together."

She thought for a minute, then blew out from her nose. "Then what? I don't know how to get along out there. Where do we go? How do we live?"

It was another question he didn't have the answer to.

She continued. "Does it really matter anyway? I'm not even worried about the future."

He thought Sharon might be right. Who's to tell if things would be better or worse? Fate, destiny, whatever you want to call it. That river is constantly changing, swirling with mud and sticks and debris and the spirits of us all. It can change, fork off, or just swirl to nowhere. Hard to swim against. The direction can shift at any time for better or worse, and that river is in no hurry. The Duration of the Struggle.

He picked up the GED study guide and gave it to her. She slid it under the mattress and smoothed out the stained sheet, telling him to go before Bob got back. The house was so quiet for once, he could hear that lighter in her room spark up before he'd made it to the front door, and as he left, she slipped across the universe.

# Eight

HE PULLED UP THE FENCING AND SLID UNDER, then looked past the moon floating in the soft light of the city, into the endless cosmos, and saw there was nothing alive but him even though the spirits of Osage Avenue followed him everywhere, constantly baiting him to join their army. He was surrounded by the stolen lives of the animals, but it didn't matter, he felt he was the only one living. He knew any one of them would have trampled him to get to the other side of the fence, yet he was clawing to get in. A ratty end of metal caught his arm and tore it open some, but he hardly felt a thing.

That night he made his way into the African exhibit, the African plains. Africa, the cradle of life. There were a few animals in there that could hurt him if they wanted. No lions or wildebeests but zebras, giraffes, a rhino. Any of them could have easily killed him. And maybe that's what he wanted.

At night it was their world again. No humans to entertain, nobody trying to pelt them with peanuts and pretzels. They spoke to each other about the familiar light of the moon, the same moon that shone over their relatives half a world away, freely walking the real African plains. They were removed from that life but still lived under its laws, the laws that were always there, Natural Law, and he was becoming one of them. An estranged sibling that they just didn't know well enough yet but instinct told them to accept as their own. Smiley said that any animal could be dangerous if it was cornered or injured, even a rabbit, because animals did what they had to do to survive. They didn't feel remorse or worry about repercussions. If they were threatened, they acted. MOVE said an animal had the right to defend itself if it felt threatened. If it *feels* threatened, not if it *is* threatened. That's an important difference. The right to defend oneself. It's a simple way of living a hard life.

He wanted to sleep right in the dirt. Right in the dust and hay and shit, to be an animal and curl up out in the open, but he was too much of a coward. There was a baobab tree in the exhibit, a massive fiberglass replica of a huge ancient tree that looks like it's growing upside down, with the leafless, lifeless root system aboveground, reaching for the sun, and the green life of the tree buried in the ground. He wedged himself into a crevice and stared at the stars in the African night. Usually the lights of the city were so bright that they smothered out the universe and only the brightest stars could make it through, but still, they were all there. Trillions of them, and if they were all visible, the whole sky would be a solid wall of blinding stars, some that have been dead for tens, even hundreds, of millions of years. They reached to the ends of the conflicted cosmos, if there were an end. And if there were an end, and even if there weren't, and it was just endlessly reaching into the black unknown beyond our comprehension, maybe he was in the exact center. At that exact moment, at that exact time, maybe he was at the exact pinpoint of the center of the universe. Who could say he wasn't?

Grunts of a large animal, its heavy feet keeping a steady pace to nowhere. Trigger grunted back, low, testing his acceptance without committing to it. The sound evaporated into the night without a response. A giraffe paced by right in front of him with long, unconcerned strides, gliding sleeplessly through the night. Giraffes sleep for only about a half hour a night, and that's about how little he felt like he had been sleeping. If they could survive on that little, he figured maybe he could too, but humans have evolved to need sleep. And he needed it.

He spent the solitary time the way he often spent his time alone, dreaming of ways to hurt Bob, to kill him even. He thought again about maybe paying one of the Thomas brothers to shoot him but figured that would probably never work out. He imagined stabbing a knife deep into Bob's chest and looking him right in the eyes as he did it, and that felt really satisfying, Bob looking into him while he, Trigger, had all the power, watching Bob's life light flicker out. But he was thin and frail while Bob was as big as a bear. Smiley once said that one time the zoo had to take a tranquilized Kodiak bear to fix a broken tooth. Shot it with a tranquilizer gun and it dropped. It got him to thinking, if that dart was big enough to take down a huge bear, it was probably enough to kill Bob. The image of his father dropping like a bear gave Trigger a moment of peace, and he drifted off at some point, with Bob's empty funeral floating at the edge of his mind.

⁂

He saw that rusted grill of the truck, again, but they didn't. The headlights like hot white eyes, ready to pounce, and he couldn't say or do anything about it. It hit, and the glass sprayed like shotgun pelt. The car crumpled in half, and they jerked and twisted in pain together, again. Then the smell of gas and the heat of the flames. Then the screaming.

⁂

Rabbit rabbit.

He had to remember.

That next morning, as he brushed his teeth in the bathroom, he considered the night before, sleeping in the dirt with the animals. Unprotected. De-wilding. He daydreamed about doing it for the rest of his life; daydreamed to the point where he forgot to wash his face. He thought he must have looked like total shit, because when Smiley saw him, the first thing he said was that Trigger looked like total shit. Smiley told him to clean himself up before the supervisor saw him.

Trigger went back to the bathroom to clean up. In the mirror Trigger saw him, that kid on the corner, Nee-Gro. Dirty blonde hair shoulder length and shaggy, hanging into his bloodshot, blue eyes. Dark circles beneath those eyes, too dark for a kid that age, and a huge red welt beneath his left eye where Bob had cracked him good. There was crusted blood all down his right arm where it had caught on the fence, and on his face where he must have rubbed it during the night. It was coated over with dust just like the rest of him.

He turned on the water and let it run, just staring into that Nee-Gro in the mirror, wishing he had burned up in that fire with the MOVE members, with Tree Africa. At least he would have stood for something, died for something, and not just been left drifting toward an unknown fate. A fate he had no control over. A fate he didn't want.

Trigger stared into that mirror until his eyes filled with water and ran down his cheeks like tiny muddy streams.

The heavy metal door pushed open, and Smiley stood in the doorway, his thin frame like a scarecrow come to life. Trigger rubbed his eyes into the small towel he pulled from his backpack, but he was glad Smiley saw him crying. He figured Smiley would ask and he would answer, and Smiley would have the solution.

Smiley stepped across the tile floor as quiet as dust, got right up next to him, speaking to him in the mirror.

"Huh . . . had a bad one, I guess?"

Trigger nodded and looked at the deep-set eyes in that dark face, two flashing black pearls in a withered old apple.

"Finish washing your face," he said. "We gotta get to work."

He didn't ask anything, just turned to leave. It was such a kick in the stomach that a bottled-up cry burped its way out of Trigger's mouth, shooting spit into the mirror and down his chin.

"But . . ." was all he was able to get out.

Smiley stopped at the door, rubbing the back of his thin neck with that huge hand, and spun back to look at him.

Filthy, crying, and lost.

"But . . . what?" he said. "But life is tough? Nobody said it was gonna be easy. But you all fucked up? But you poor? But . . . but . . . but . . . Don't bring that *but* shit to me. You got a problem, you gotta fix it, ain't no one else in this world gonna do it for you. The sooner you learn that my son, the sooner you stop crying in the mirror. Every one of those animals out there got their problems, every day. They deal with it, and you will too."

He stepped up to Trigger and laid that hand on his shoulder, soft but still heavy as lead.

"Listen. I know it's tough. I know you got it bad sometimes. But you gotta handle it. Most of the shit people have to deal with, they can deal with. But if you get in too deep, you always got Uncle Sam here."

He blew out through his flat nose, frustrated, like he knew he wasn't getting his point across.

"What I'm sayin' is, if all the people you know put all their problems on the table, and you got to take any ones you wanted, you'd probably take your own ones back. That's how it works. You get what you can take. You can fold up, suck back in like a little turtle, and sit there waiting for things to get safe, or you can stretch out like a motherfucking lion and roar and take no shit off nobody. You gonna get a scar, you gonna get bitten, but everyone gotta get tested. Ain't nobody given anything, you gotta earn it."

He spun Trigger around by the backpack, so he was looking square into his weathered eyes. The serious look melted away, and that huge smile spread across his face, with all those teeth showing, the pink gums like strawberry ice cream against his black skin.

"Now," he nodded, "you a man or you a mouse? Squeak up!" With that he laughed loud and deep. It bounced against the cool tile walls of the bathroom, relentless and booming like the unseen waves of a giant ringing bell. That smile, that sound, it had nowhere else to go but into Trigger. It soaked in through his skin and ears, beyond his control, and without realizing it, he was laughing too. Not nearly as hard, barely making a sound, but it was there, a real, genuine laugh, something he thought couldn't come from within him.

That afternoon he skipped lunch with Smiley. Their break was the same time the lions and tigers got fed, and Trigger wanted to be there. They were fed inside, in a long concrete corridor, behind black iron bars like those of an old western prison cell, each with their own cell so they wouldn't fight over the food. They paced, knowing it was close, the corridor thick as always with people waiting to watch them. When the keeper showed up with that bucket of meat, the roar those animals let out barreled down the hall like a thunderstorm. The tigers were so powerful and so aggressive; even though they were behind bars, it seemed like they were in charge. They shouted and the keeper responded. They tore into the meat, leaving red stains on their wide paws and around their mouths. Although imprisoned, they still seemed just as strong as in the wild, and Trigger stood awed by that power.

After the feeding, most of the cats made their way back outside to lay in the summer sun, but one tiger stayed behind. Most of the people left too, but Trigger stayed. That one tiger kept pacing, one side to the other, the tip of his tail brushing each wall as he spun. He had eaten. He had made his voice heard, but he still paced, he still wanted something else. Trigger didn't know what it was. It roared, and its nose wrinkled, eyes bright and alive but unsatisfied. Trigger felt the roar vibrate in his chest. Aggravated and serious. It was looking right at him. Speaking to him alone.

He thought about what that would be like, feeding Bob to the animals. But that was just a daydream, and he needed a real solution.

Toward the end of the day, Smiley radioed Trigger to meet up at the prairie dog exhibit, in the holding room. There was almost always some kind of holding area behind each exhibit, for animals that were new to get acclimated, or for injured animals to heal up, or for the animals to have routine checkups. Trigger had to bring in two bales of hay and set up a new pen since one of the prairie dogs was soon to give birth. Trigger had seen a few smaller animals give birth, but the prairie dog would be the biggest, and it wasn't even that big at all.

After they'd set up the pen, they brought her in and she scratched around a bit, fluffing up an area where she then settled. The keeper said she would be ready in just a few days.

That day Trigger left the zoo by the main gates. He rarely left by the front, not wanting to fight through the strollers and swarms of kids running in circles, but the prairie dog exhibit was near that exit, and he spent the little time left on his shift watching that prairie dog in the pen.

Outside the heavy front gates, standing on a wooden crate, was a man with a red bullhorn. Long, tight dreadlocks twisted out from beneath a red, yellow, green, and black rastacap. He was shirtless, his dark skin pulled tight over the wiry muscles beneath, like he had been worked too hard for too long, with too little to eat. He glistened, and clouds gathered over him and the sweat he wore like a coat of pride. He reeled back and forth, screaming at the crowd leaving the zoo. His eyes nearly glowed red, and his voice crackled with rage as he spit into the bullhorn. He was screaming so loud, and the speaker was so distorted, that Trigger caught only pieces of his rant. It was about how everyone there was contributing to slavery, how each one of them was a part of the problem and that they would burn, just like the MOVE house had burned.

Young parents pushed their children right past him, like he was invisible, like they had a clear bubble around them and the words bounced off. He was above all of them, hovering over the rush of people getting back to their cars as the clouds started to drizzle. They flowed around him like he was a huge rock in a black river that the water split in half to avoid.

Trigger locked into him, hypnotized. Trigger was the only one who heard the man, and it seemed like he was speaking directly to him. He squinted those red eyes, glassy and on fire. His nose wrinkled, just like that caged tiger. His voice was full of hell, cursing all of them, even Trigger. "Hey, you!" he shouted, eyes beaming right into Trigger's. Trigger twisted his head to both sides, then pointed to his chest, asking if he was talking to him, pointing right into his zoo shirt, the one all the employees wore.

"Yea you, motherfucker. You work here? You a goddamn slave owner! Who the fuck are you to be keeping animals locked up?"

Trigger dropped his mouth to say something, but he was so scared he froze. Heat was pouring out of the man's mouth, out of his soul, radiating directly at Trigger, and it paralyzed him solid.

People continued to ignore the man and his bullhorn, ignore Trigger and his helplessness, and he stood there terrified for reasons he wasn't even entirely sure of. He was locked up, and hardly a breath of air could make it into his lungs.

"How 'bout I lock your ass up in a cage? Let me take your freedom away! You better than them? What makes you think you got the goddamn right to feed them when you want? Clean them when you want? These animals here for your entertainment? That's not what we believe! Long live John Africa! This is slavery! Down with this goddamn system! Long live John Africa! Fuck this system! Get ready for a war cause it's gonna be a tough goddamn war!"

He shouted and cursed into the bullhorn, so close to people's ears it scratched at their brains. But they refused to look at him. They refused to even acknowledge he existed, that Trigger existed.

The clouds got heavy, and a cool rain soon replaced the drizzle, sizzling on the pavement and the man's anger. People ducked from the drops as they scrambled away, and the viciousness in the man's voice flattened out. His chest heaved as he caught his breath. He pulled the bullhorn away and spoke directly to Trigger without it, still just as angry. Not like he was doing it for himself, like he was doing it for others. Like he knew something no one else did and he was telling it to him so Trigger would understand. Trigger stood there paralyzed, getting soaked, eyes locked on the Rasta's until the crowd was gone and the man finally stepped down, turned his back. Then he turned around just once more, megaphone still held tight in his hand but held to his hip.

"All praise to the order of life . . . I'm talkin' 'bout freedom . . . goddammit. You know the difference between right and wrong, don't you? You think it's right, what's going on in there? You think those animals would rather be there than in the wild? Let me tell you something else . . ." He stretched a painful grimace across his face, lifted a skinny worn finger, and pointed it at Trigger, about to spear him directly in the heart, and Trigger braced for it, hypnotized and unable to look away.

The rain picked up just a bit, and they were the only two left outside the zoo, locked into each other. The man dropped his finger as if losing his train of thought, then ran his finger through his dreadlocks. "Long live John Africa," he said in a flat voice, and turned away. He picked up the crate and walked off with his back rigid, head up to the sky for the rain to shower his face.

Trigger, free from his spell, couldn't shake the feeling that maybe he was right, maybe that man knew Trigger better than he knew himself. He *did* work at the zoo, contributing to the imprisonment of the animals he loved. He needed the zoo. He needed the animals. Maybe it was in his best interest to keep them there, even though he loved them and knew they were supposed to be in the wild, free.

As the man walked off and Trigger watched his naked, sinewy back slick with rain, he wanted to run to him. He wanted to ask him what he should do, what was the right thing to do. It was like he was leaving with all of the answers that Trigger needed to survive, that Sharon needed to survive, but how was that possible?

The Rasta carried away an idea, fading into the gray rain of the city, leaving Trigger feeling as gutted and empty as the homes on Osage Avenue.

He stopped at the corner store on his way home, heavy with water and guilt. The rain accelerated, a summer thunderstorm, quick and fierce, trying to wash clean the memories of the city. He cautiously pulled bills from the strap of his backpack before entering, making sure no one watched him do it. He bought a sandwich and ate half in the cover of the store's doorway, stuffing the other half into his backpack for Sharon. By the time he made it to the house, the storm had just about passed, changing to a soft, light rain, almost pleasant, though he was soaked, joints feeling cold and feet numb.

Two of the ashen drugged dead lay sprawled on that filthy brown couch, two he had never seen before. They looked up at him, but their eyes were so far away they couldn't have reached him if they had wanted to. Up the stairs, he leaned into Sharon's room to give her the sandwich, but she wasn't there so he left it on the dresser for her. She had to be in the bathroom, given the wood nailed on both the bedroom and bathroom door frames that limited her chair from getting to the hallway. He peeked from the corner of his eye as he passed on the way to his room. There she was, struggling to get from the toilet to her chair. He didn't want to, but he found himself stopping, watching her fight, watching her exhausting battle for dignity. Her thin white arms out of that shear gown, pushing with all she had. The stink of what she had just done still hanging in the air, hanging on her.

When she got into the chair, she looked up and put on a frail smile, then rolled back to her bedroom. He looked at the hinges on the door frame, thick with paint and the pins still in them. The hinges were on the interior of the jamb, with the missing door supposed to swing into the bathroom rather than out into the narrow hallway. On the outside of the jamb was the wood Bob nailed on to keep her chair from making it into the hallway. Trigger ran his finger along the wood, and his blood got hot with anger, and his eyes glowed as red and righteous as the Rasta's eyes, burning off the chill in his body. Trigger dropped his backpack right there in the hall and flew down the steps in three bounds.

Through the empty kitchen, he went out onto the covered rear porch, green paint peeling from the deck and rails. There, stacked up against the wall behind a heap of boxes and scraps of decking lumber, were three doors. He kicked the boxes into the yard and pushed the lumber aside, then pulled the first door off the stack. It was awkward maneuvering it through the kitchen door and into the house. He struggled with the weight of the solid wood as he lugged it upstairs, the dead turning their heads in unison to watch.

He couldn't make it all the way up the stairs without stopping to catch his breath. When he got it up to the bathroom, his thin arms were quivering, only to find it was the wrong door and hinged on the opposite side, so he propped it against the wall in his room, took a deep breath and let it out, then slogged down again, dragging up the second door on the deck. Again he had to stop halfway up the steps, resting his head on the door, muttering to himself as he panted. He was so exhausted from the entire day, he didn't think he could make it, but it was further to go back than to continue on.

This one fit. It didn't fit tight, and the handle didn't work, but he managed to get it to close. At least there was a door on the bathroom, and he didn't care what Bob was going to do about it.

He peeled off his soaking clothes and hung them around his room to dry. The rain had cooled off the city, but it was still so muggy it was hard to breathe, and the poison from downstairs wafted up the stairs and into his room, contaminating the oxygen he sucked in.

He opened the one working window in his room, propping it open with the stick he kept nearby just for that, letting in the damp early evening air and the murmurs of the city beneath him. He put on a dry pair of shorts and lay on that bare, spotted mattress, thinking he'd at least done one good thing that day, but the accusations of the Rasta at the zoo tried to smother it out. He lay with his forearm across his eyes, working out the details of the day as the overcast daylight disappeared, the hum of the city helping him find some much-needed sleep.

He woke up with a foot to his ribs and Bob stooping over him, shirtless and as hairy as a caveman. Trigger rose and they stood, both near naked and face to face, his hairless skin to Bob's fur. Bob seemed a bit smaller, the meth sucking some of the size from his chest. He looked gray and exhausted. He tried to argue, but he was so fucked up he couldn't form a complete sentence he just kept pointing back toward the hall, toward the bathroom and spitting out half words. Grabbing Trigger's arm, he pulled him toward it. Trigger broke free and followed him on his own.

"What's this?" Bob slurred.

Groggy and irritated, Trigger said it was a door.

"No," Bob said. "No . . . no doors."

"It's a bathroom," Trigger snapped. "It needs a door. People need doors." Bob's fists balled up, and Trigger tightened his sinewy muscles, ready to take the shot. Instead, Bob butted the door with his thick head, knocking it open. Through the bathroom Sharon could be seen in the doorway to the bedroom.

Bob took his fist, like a steel ball on the end of a chain, and smashed it into the thick wood panel of the door with a snap, then rested his head against it, working his fists into it like a boxer into a heavy bag, strong blows starting from his hips. It cracked but held in place. After a minute—and probably ten or twelve punches—he was winded. The knuckles on his right hand were bleeding, the hard black scabs had torn off, and there were smears of blood on the door's faded white paint. He pulled back and turned to Trigger, gasping and hunched like a fighter in the late rounds. He took one slow swing at him that Trigger easily ducked. Bob stood puffing in front of him, and Trigger stood solid, expanding his thin chest and shoulders, feeling as if he were growing larger and Bob were shrinking. Bob staggered back down the stairs, the dead watching him as he disappeared into his basement spider hole.

# Nine

THOSE HEADS SNAPPED TO THE LEFT, AND HE was jolted along with them, only difference was that he was buckled in. The glass showered over them, and the flames worked their way from the front to the rear, clawing and hungry. Terrible screaming, and the heat of the fire woke him, like it did every morning.

❧

Rabbit rabbit.

The rain of the night helped him sleep solidly for the first time in what seemed an eternity. Thoughts of his small victory the previous night came back to him, and he let them replay over and over. Bob pounding his fists into the door and wearing himself out, giving up. Smeared blood, and the fact that the door was still there.

The rain had cleared and now the sun poured through the window, along with the steam. The familiar street voices prepared for the day.

The mattress stuck to his sweaty back, but he didn't care. Even though he had the day off from the zoo, he still woke up in a good mood. Most people enjoy their time off from work, but any time he spent at the house caused stress and could lead to an explosion. Even more so, Trigger didn't like leaving Sharon there for Bob to do whatever he wanted with her. But he didn't have the stomach to stay there and watch it either, so he took the coward's way out and left, just like that car full of black faces that rolled by when Will and Troy were crowding in on him.

The work clothes from yesterday hadn't yet dried, so he left them in the room where the heat pouring in from the open window would dry them soon enough. He didn't like leaving the house without them because that meant he had to come back again, but he didn't want to spend the day with wet clothes in his pack.

These were the things he had to think about on summer break, while other kids were concerned only with what they would be taking to the pool that day and what friends they might see there.

Walking past the bathroom door smeared with Bob's blood made him smile, but that evaporated in an instant as he looked into the bedroom and saw her motionless, pinned beneath Bob's heavy arm. He snored so loudly she couldn't possibly have been sleeping, and Trigger was sure she was just lying there awake, paralyzed twice over. Just that arm draped over her stirred such an anger in him that he stepped into the room to pull it off but froze, backing out quietly and slipping sheepishly down the stairs. One of the near-dead was still on the couch, sitting up either asleep or still so high he couldn't keep his eyes open. He sat there, filthy, fading into the brown fabric.

Even though it was still early, the humidity was already stifling. The black streets and red brick buildings siphoned in the heat, holding it so not a wisp of fresh air seemed to blow down Osage Avenue. The rowhouses closed in, towering over the black river of macadam, every one of them stuffed with losses and unease, victories and dreams.

Before Trigger even realized it, he had wandered back to the MOVE house. Most of the bigger debris was gone, but the ground was still thick with charred wood and ash; metal skeletons of wire and pipe were the only proof of prior lives. The tall brick walls that stood between each home were braced with wood to keep them from falling over, and the fresh tan wood stood out like bleached bone against the backdrop of the scorched earth.

Trigger again sat on the stoop across the street, staring into the past and thinking about the Rasta from the zoo he had seen the day before. He wanted to see him again, and he didn't even really know why. Something just felt unresolved. He *did* see Troy Thomas; the thick puffy afro and light skin made him noticeable from a block away. He was alone, without Will, which gave Trigger some relief. He walked by on the dead side of the street in front of the yellow caution tape. He looked right at Trigger but kept on going.

After minutes or hours, the owner of the home came out and politely told Trigger to get off his stoop. Trigger left and went to the library to get a few books on animals for both himself and Sharon, then spent the rest of the day wandering. Past the corner store where he always went, the same fixtures of locals passing time standing out front scratching lottery tickets and smoking. Past the old ladies in the laundromat sitting behind the metal screening that protects the large glass windows.

There were always people on the stoops of their homes and on the porches, some drinking beers as the music from their radios drifted down the block. Kids his age and younger heading to the park, bouncing a basketball in the middle of the street, then darting onto the sidewalk when a car came. Before the bombing, even the MOVE children would sometimes be out there, playing with neighborhood children in the street or in front yards, and sometimes at the park as well. There was constant activity, always people living their lives. It was a community, and still was, one he was part of whether he realized it or not. Mostly black, a few Hispanic, and fewer white, like him.

He could walk for hours between his house, Osage Avenue, the zoo, and the library. He didn't mind. He had nothing else to do. He never thought about how much time he spent alone, it was just his lot in life, how things were, but it was almost all day, every day. His body moved on autopilot, navigating streets, watching normal people going about their everyday business and the near-dead in the neighborhood, all without thinking or making conscious decisions, like the ghosts of the MOVE house. They all drifted together, pulled to nowhere by an unseen, all-powerful force. He talked only to himself, in his head. Conversations and questions that he didn't have enough knowledge of the world to answer. Some that no one had the answers to.

By the time he made it back to the house to give Sharon the books, the day had begun to cool, just enough to be able to stand without sweating. But inside the house it was stagnant and dark, the lives within adding to the heat. Halfway up the stairs to her bedroom, he saw the bathroom door was gone again, and he slammed his palm onto the wood handrail, cursing out loud as it slapped. He gave the books to Sharon, and she said Bob was in a bad mood.

"I'm in a bad mood too," he said. "I'm always in a bad mood."

"No," she said, "something went wrong. Something went wrong with what he's doing. With who he's been dealing with."

Trigger told her not to worry about it and that he would take care of it, but he had no idea what she was even talking about.

He went into the backyard and found the door lying on the ground, thrown onto the concrete slab yard. He picked it up and awkwardly dragged it back into the house to the stairs, where Bob was standing after just leaving the basement. He held his thick palm against the door, strong enough to stop Trigger from moving up the stairs.

"Put it back," Bob said flatly. He had a shirt on at least, and jeans, but no shoes. His eyes were tired, more tired than usual, hazed from years of deterioration.

"It's a door," Trigger said. "It's supposed to be in the bathroom. She doesn't want people looking in on her."

Bob let go of the door and dropped his eyes, looking to the floor and shaking his head as if Trigger had just answered a question wrong.

"Where do you get off? Where the hell do you get off making changes around here? This is my house, understand? My house, my rules. If I want the goddamn door off, the door is off."

"It's not right. We're people, not animals."

Trigger started up the stairs. Bob shoved the door into him with both hands, knocking Trigger against the wall and snapping his head back so that it hit the plaster. Trigger shook it off, took a deep breath in through his nose, and took another step up the stairs. Again Bob pushed, and again Trigger shook it off and stepped up. Hands to door, head to wall. He wouldn't be the first to give in. This went on until they were at the top of the stairs and Trigger's head was ringing.

Sharon had rolled her chair to the door frame and watched the struggle from her room. Trigger dragged the door to the bathroom, body tight and ready at any moment to get a punch or smack. Bob puffed up, looking about to explode, but the effort seemed too much for his decaying body. He blew all the rage out from his mouth.

"Ahh, fuck it anyway," he said, and teetered back downstairs.

The bathroom had a door again.

Trigger went to his room, where the wrong door from the day before was still propped up against the wall. He pulled the pins from the hinges on the jamb and lifted the door into place, struggling to hold the weight of the solid door while working to marry the intricate pieces of the hinge together and slide a pin back in at the same time. It fit the door frame, and he had a door again too. He wanted to shut it and just be in his own world, as small as his world was, but he saw Sharon in the doorway of her room, still with no door of her own, so he left it open.

That night the house began to fill up with the dead, more than usual. Mixed in with the regulars were two others, two who looked cleaner and more focused. Both black and serious, they seemed to be there for a reason other than drying up and hiding from their lives. Bob took them into the basement, pulling off the heavy brass padlock. Music drifted through the house like smoke. When Trigger checked on Sharon, she was somehow asleep in her chair, looking twisted and uncomfortable. He helped her into bed and stacked the books on the table by the window. The hamster fidgeted, unaware of the lives outside its cage. Trigger reached in and pulled it out, its pink feet tickling the palm of his hand. He held it to his face, rubbing its soft fur against his cheek, and he found himself whispering to it, just as he had seen Smiley and Sharon do, whispering to it that everything was fine, that it would be fine, unsure if he was telling that to the hamster or if he was pretending that the hamster was telling it to him.

With Sharon asleep in her pen and the dead piling in, he got his now-dry zoo uniform and stuffed it into the backpack. He picked his way through the rotting dead to the front door, and there, outside on the chipped concrete stoop, was Will Thomas.

Will sat facing the street, throwing pebbles at a can on the sidewalk. It reminded Trigger of when Will threw pebbles at the zebra in the zoo and what happened when he, Trigger, had tried stopping him.

Will plunked the can once, then whipped the rest in his hand at a car parked in the street. The pebbles hit like shotgun spray and fell to the concrete. Trigger tried to slip by him unnoticed, which was impossible.

"Hey Nee-Gro . . . where you goin', boy?" Will jumped up from the stoop and got close, his face so near, Trigger could see every pimple busting through the black surface, reminding him that Will was just a boy, like himself. He could smell some kind of coconut scent oozing out from beneath that backward hat. Rich and powerful, the delicious tropical scent drifted across the indifferent concrete in his vision, scrambling wires in Trigger's brain. Will's eyes came only up to Trigger's nose, but he felt like Will was looking down on him, not the other way around. Looking down on him from ten feet above.

When Trigger didn't answer, Will lowered his head and knocked shoulders, like he always did.

"You wanna give it a go?"

Will sprung back and started throwing fast jabs in the air around Trigger's head, striking within inches of his face with the speed and accuracy of a snake. The sleeves of his shirt popped against his arm. He ducked and bobbed, boxing against a rigid partner, his breath pushing out between his clenched teeth with each punch he threw. Even as he danced around Trigger's back, leaving him prone to anything Will wanted to do, Trigger stood frozen in fear. When Will got around to Trigger's front again, he dropped his right hand low while holding his left fist up high and twirling it in the air, and Trigger kept his eyes on that left hand.

"Wham!" Will shouted, swinging a huge hook with his right hand at Trigger's head. Trigger only had time to wince and shut his eyes. He heard Will laugh, and Trigger opened his eyes to see Will's fist stopped within an inch of his temple and Will's fiercely grinning expression.

"That's the one!" he yelled. "That's the one gonna drop you!"

Will bounced a few steps back, fists guarding his face, elbows in close to his body, and chin tucked down into his neck, still bobbing and rolling his shoulders up tight.

"Will," a voice called from the door to the house. It was one of the clean-looking guys who had followed Bob into the basement. He nodded his head upward on a thin neck in a clean-collared shirt, beckoning Will, and Will nodded back and bounded up the steps in two strides, leaving the scent of coconut hanging in the air behind him.

All the way to the zoo, Trigger hated himself for closing his eyes when Will threw that feint. The walk gave him nothing but time to think. Always too much time to think. Baddest motherfucking animal in the zoo, Smiley said.

He slipped in under the fence behind the wolf habitat, back in with the animals where he belonged. The wolf habitat was on the south side of the zoo, next to the cheetah exhibit, at the 34th Street entrance. Between there and the entrance gates on the north end were all of the exhibits, animals, and sanctuaries he could ask for. The zoo was his home, and his choices were many.

He wanted to go sleep with the prairie dog, but he was so upset with himself that he feared passing along that upset to the pregnant female. He went back into the tortoise pen instead, his actions—or inactions—with Will Thomas engulfing him like a poisonous fog. He would have felt better about himself if he'd kept his eyes open and Will had hit him, rather than just closing them and doing nothing.

Floating down the paths, through the trees and shrubs, across the grass, leaving no footprints in the hot dew, invisible to the universe, a shadow of a ghost. The moon's soothing white light bathed him in its pity. The tortoises didn't even want him. They don't feel emotion. A distant cousin that didn't know him and didn't want to. They stretched their necks out, peering around the boulders, their small brains confused as to why another animal would deliberately choose captivity. They scratched in the dirt, pinning Trigger in. A zoo within a zoo. He lay quietly, waiting for them to get distracted by something else and move along, which they eventually did.

Maybe he slept, maybe not, it was hard to tell, but he stayed there with eyes closed, alone with the moonlight pouring over him like skim milk, the conflicted universe watching it all unfold.

He smelled the age of the tortoises, and he was aging with them, close to rotting into the ground. He didn't stand up for himself against Will, and this was his way of punishing himself. The tortoise pen was safe, but it stunk and was uncomfortable. He knew the hay with the prairie dog was clean and fresh, and it didn't take very long for him to forgive himself. Rather than waste away with the tortoises, he got up and decided to go see the pregnant prairie dog, hoping to sleep next to it like one of its coming pups.

The master key slipped easily into the lock and he was in. It was spooky dark, at least for him, with one light at the end of the hall casting a dull yellow glow down the corridor. He felt his way, dragging fingertips along the smooth walls, following the scent of the hay. The pen he headed toward was only about six feet by six feet, with three walls that went to the ceiling. The front wall was only about five feet high, with a latched door like a horse stall. The light was just enough to see into the pen where the prairie dog lay curled up in a ball, nestled in the safe hay. Trigger stood as quietly as possible, watching it sleep, its back slightly heaving with each breath, and he wondered if it was dreaming of wide-open spaces, of other places, or if animals even dreamed at all. He went into the pen and approached it, crawling through the hay on his hands and knees. He wanted to lie beside it, that mother about to give birth, knowing its instinct would have it do all it could in its power to protect its young, once born. It flinched without waking and he froze, then crawled to the opposite corner of the pen and curled up in the hay. It smelled earthy, familiar. The prairie dog woke and lifted its head, sniffing toward him, but it lay back down, sensing there wasn't a threat. Just a pup looking for a safe place to sleep.

He saw that prairie dog as a cute, furry little animal that he wanted to get close to, to be taken in by, but like most things in Trigger's life, it wasn't as it seemed. Infanticide is a somewhat common occurrence in prairie dog life. A female family member will kill the young of other females so that her pups have a greater chance of survival, so that her own children thrive. Murdering the other young for the benefit of her own.

Backpack pillow. He fell asleep fast, mind fixed on the problems that we animals all have.

♣

Rabbit rabbit.

He could have been asleep for fifteen minutes or five hours, he didn't know, but it was still dark. When he woke up, his stomach twisted with pain, reminding him that he had eaten almost nothing the entire day and had forgotten to pick up a sandwich or to stop at the snack shack while creeping through the zoo earlier that night. He brushed the hay off and put on the backpack to go out and forage for some food with the rest of the nocturnal animals.

The gloomy light in the corridor threw a long shadow that headed to the exit. When he opened the door and stepped out into the night, right there, leaning against the wall directly next to the door, beneath the insects dancing around the light fixture, was a security guard smoking a cigarette. The guard jumped back, startled as much as he had startled Trigger. A cigarette hung from his lips, and the smoke billowed across a face speckled with tiny black dots. He was tall and wiry, a light-skinned black like Troy Thomas.

"Jesus!" He reached for his belt, but the only thing it held was his walkie-talkie. "What the fuck you doin' in there?"

He shook off the surprise, took a long draw from his smoke, pinched it between his thumb and index finger, then flicked it. The glowing end disappeared into the night. He pulled the radio from his belt, ready to call it in.

"Wait," Trigger pleaded, "I work here."

"Scared me half to goddamn death. You what? You work here? Watchu doing in there in the middle of the goddamn night? What's your name?"

He kept his finger on the button of the radio, holding it close to his head.

"I'm Trey. I work with Smiley."

"You work with Smiley?"

He leaned in closer, squinting his dark eyes and wrinkling his leathery face. Trigger recognized him, recognized those dark spots, like a crop of tiny black mushrooms popping out of his caramel skin. He was friends with Smiley, but everybody seemed to be. Trigger remembered him having lunch with them a few times. His name was Myles, or Charles, he couldn't remember for sure. Smiley said he was a retired Philadelphia cop, and you wouldn't know it to look at him, but he used to be the toughest son of a bitch in the city. He was an enforcer and a head cracker for Frank Rizzo when Rizzo was the chief of police. Rizzo ruled with an iron hand, and this guard had been part of his crew.

"Oh yeah, I remember you," he dropped the radio to his hip and they both relaxed a bit, though Trigger remained wary. "Still don't explain what you doin' in there in the middle of the goddamn night."

Trigger had thought many times what he would say if he were to ever get caught in the zoo after closing. Hours of seclusion and thinking. Now it was here, and he had nothing prepared. He just went with what popped into his head.

"I fell asleep. I fell asleep at work today, at the end of the day. When I woke up, the zoo was closed. I didn't know what to do." His breathing was shallow and quick, and the blood pumped through his veins, forcing him awake. "Please don't tell Smiley. I didn't mean it."

The guard rubbed his chin with the radio and thought. "All right, all right . . . just calm down."

He considered what Trigger said. "Still don't explain how you got into this here building."

There were only a certain number of master keys, and the guard had one, so he knew that too.

"I helped Smiley set up the pen for the prairie dog. I just wanted to go look at it. The door was unlocked."

He nodded his head and grinned. "How is Uncle Sam? He still dreaming about San Diego?"

Trigger said yes, and with that he felt the pressure release like air from a balloon. The guard walked him to the front gate with his hand on Trigger's shoulder. At first the guard asked if he needed to use a phone to call his parents, but Trigger lied and said he lived right around the corner.

"You okay walking home alone, through this town? West Philly can be a tough place."

He said it was fine. The guard unlocked the front turnstile beside the main iron gates, and he was out. He heard the guard whistling as he casually strolled back into the zoo, like a kindly old grandfather without a care, his violent history a lifetime away, a history belonging to someone else.

Trigger checked his watch. 3:10. He must have slept much longer than he'd figured. He was exhausted, never seeming to get a full night's sleep. Always so tired. The neighborhood was empty save for the sentinel streetlights that quietly and constantly observed everything. Along with the pale moon, they cast long shadows onto the black macadam. He was afraid of the type of people he might run into: degenerates, castaways, the forgotten, the type of people who were out at that hour, but the street was a black hole of nothingness and no one. The more he walked alone, the clearer it became, he was the only one out on those dark streets. The only twig drifting in a muddy river.

The house was quiet when he arrived. Up the stairs he could see Sharon sleeping alone, and that made him feel better. He closed the newly hung door to his room and collapsed onto the mattress.

Just before dawn, just as the morning light began to filter into the room but with it still feeling like night, a thumping woke him. He was crusted with sleep, but the sound drew him in. The moth to the light. He didn't want to know, but he knew. He pulled his door open and crept down the hall on the balls of his feet. Before he even got there, he knew. The first thing he saw were her feet. So pale, rubbing on the floor lifelessly. He got just a bit closer. There she was, bent over the bed, feet and dead legs hanging from the edge and the part of her body that could feel pressed face down on the sheets, white on white. Bob was behind her, completely naked, that key hanging from the long chain around his neck slapping against her bony back. Her rubber legs swayed and scraped on the floor. She clung onto the mattress for some type of support as he held her hips with his ape-like hands. Right at that moment, Trigger pictured the gun Troy Thomas kept in his waistband, and he wished he had it right then. If it were in his clammy hand, he would have killed all three of them right there, Sharon first, then Bob, then himself. He thought it, and he meant it. He thought of finding something to smash over Bob's head, but then she would know what he'd seen, and he couldn't let her know that. And he couldn't go down the steps to leave; they would hear. He could only slink back to his room and wrap his head in a dirty shirt and try to fall back to sleep, wishing the MOVE house was still standing so he could hear them, so the words and ideals pumping from that loudspeaker could push everything else from his mind.

# Ten

Sometimes people say they recall trauma happening in slow motion, but for Trigger it was more like stop motion, like drawing dozens of stick figures on index cards and then flicking through them, watching them jerk around like marionettes at the mercy of their master.

❧

Trigger had been complaining from the back seat the entire ride, ignored and forgotten, but now he was pestering his mother about something so repeatedly and so annoyingly that he had her rattled. She was dealing with a whole world of other issues—relationships, responsibilities, financial struggles—and he was just piling on, concerned only with the issues in *his* world, like children often are. Like many people are.

She kept craning her neck around to yell at him, telling him to *quiet down*, and when she got exhausted from that, she just stared straight ahead through the windshield as he continued needling her.

He had a stuffed animal on his lap, an owl, with big yellow plastic eyes. When she wouldn't turn back around to give him the attention he wanted, he threw it at her. Hit her right in the side of the head and knocked her glasses off. That got the reaction he had waited for, and she leaned half her body over the seat to shut him up, to see what was so important. As she was stretching around, giving in to his needs, his wants, they blew right through that light.

The grill of that truck was heavy with rust, but beefy and rugged, as if it had driven countless hard miles in all kinds of bad weather and was pissed off. Sharon and their mother didn't see it, they were both looking at Trigger, away from the windows, but he saw it. It was heading right for the driver's side, right between them in the front and back seats, and he had a clear look at that big grill. The glass from the windows burst in, showering them, and they were all weightless for a second. His mom and Sharon were jolted together, both moving in unison, folded at the waist with heads snapping to the left in synchrony, as if practicing a morbid dance. The metal groaned and twisted, and the whole left side of the car crumpled. Trigger was in a booster seat, and it held strong, buckled into the car and yanking him back, preventing him from being thrown through the windshield. But neither Sharon nor his mother had seat belts on.

When the car finally settled, the smell of gasoline was suffocating. That's the sharpest memory he held, the smell of the gas, then the burning rubber and plastic. The car didn't burst into flames, it just caught and then burned from the engine back into the car with a venom, like it hated his mother and wanted her to suffer, and she did. The smoke rolled over them and there was nothing but screaming and choking on that smoke, the rest of the world blacked out.

⁂

Rabbit rabbit.

Keep trying.

He woke up with the shirt still wrapped around his head, drenched in sweat from the heat or the dream or both. The morning sun poured in through the shadeless, clouded windows of the room, holding in the heat like the snake tanks at the zoo. They were always peaceful, those first few seconds of waking up, when the day before hadn't crept back into his thoughts, before his life flooded back into him. The dreams of the night evaporated from his mind before he could see them in the light, but then the past came billowing back. The security guard. Will Thomas at the house. Bob and Sharon.

He wished he could live just in those first few seconds of each morning.

Trigger had to be at work by noon. He packed up to head out, and at the end of the hall he saw Sharon working her rubbery legs into jeans, no Bob. He went partway down the staircase and leaned over so he could see the basement door. The lock was on, so Bob was out of the house. Sharon lay flat on the bed, pulling the jeans up and moving her legs around with her arms to wriggle them in, her hair draped in front of her face. She called to him, just called out *Trey*, not hello or help, just his name. He went to her, and smelled the burning smell of plastic. She made her way into the chair and spun it to the dresser with the hamster cage on it. She rattled her fingernail lightly across the cage. "What's it like outside?"

"It's hot."

She took up the pipe and stuffed some crystals in. The flame from the lighter was high, close to her face as she crooked her neck to hit it, and the light caught the wrinkles of a young woman trapped in an older, beaten body. The smoke wisped around her head, a silhouette against the yellow smoke filmed on the window's glass. She held it in, and without looking back, held her limp white hand across her body, offering the pipe to him without speaking.

He had smoked pot before and had even caught Smiley smoking it once after work at the zoo, but Trigger had never smoked meth. He was afraid to. He saw how people changed, physically changed into something else, someone else. More than that, he was afraid he would like it.

"Smoke with me," she said without turning from the window. "Sit here, smoke with me."

At that point he wanted to be someone else, or to at least forget who he was. Where he was. He saw the constant flow of street dead, high and seemingly without a care for where they were or what was to come. It was a temporary solution that turned into a permanent problem for some, but at least, he figured, they had moments without worry. It was a break from reality, not a solution to their problems. But at that point, a break was better than nothing. Like those first few seconds when he woke up in the morning.

He took the backpack off and sat on the bed, in the same place where just a few hours ago he'd watched Bob fucking her as hard as he could, as violently as he could, and he wanted to forget, and if that was what it was going to take, then that's what he would do. Sharon pulled the pipe away from her dry, chapped lips. He took that pipe from her scabbed hand. It felt more warm than hot, almost comfortable. Smooth: It actually felt like it fit perfectly into his hand. He pressed the tip against his lips, where hers had just been, she turned to him and sparked the lighter, and it flashed close to his eyes. He drew in and felt the pipe get hot at his lips and the fog roll down his throat, as hot and dry as the dust in the African exhibit. He held, and it pushed, forcing its way back out of his lungs. He coughed so hard the crystals shook out of that purple glass pipe and spilled onto the blackened hardwood floor, and they both watched the orange embers quickly fade dark. She packed it again and he hit it again, this time harder. It was harsher than the first hit, and he coughed violently again, but this time she took the pipe out of his hand and drew from it. Back and forth. He lost count. Flash. He had never been on a roller coaster, but he imagined this is what it would feel like, a rush of steaming straight down, not knowing what was going to happen, his heart pumping so fast he didn't care, just wanting to enjoy it. The anticipation of the climb, wondering what was just on the other side of that peak, then the terrifying drop. The possibility that things could go terribly wrong but the rush almost euphoric.

Sharon threw her head back, and her hair fell from her face. She wasn't laughing, but she wasn't crying either. Trigger sat for a minute and his body felt as if it were doubling in size, sucking up all the oxygen in the room, and he worried that she might pass out from lack of air.

"Get me out of this place," she said. "Take me outside."

Before that moment, he would have never thought he was strong enough or big enough to pick up anyone, being just a bony fourteen-year-old, but he had a new feeling inside, like he had grown so large that he didn't even question it. It felt good. Different. A power he had been seeking for a very long time. He pushed her chair to the door, and the wheels bumped into the trim Bob had put up, just enough so the chair wouldn't go, locking her in.

She asked him to squat in front of her, then she wrapped her arms around his neck and he stood, her warm body and light bones on his back, hollow like a small bird, the only things separating their skin were their thin T-shirts. He scooped up a limp leg in each arm, locking his fingers together at his stomach, and carried her down the stairs. He felt like he could have carried ten of her.

The stairs groaned under their combined weight. That familiar sound. Beyond the bolted basement door, past the battered couch and marred floor, they went out into the sun of the day. He walked across the porch and down a few steps, then squatted down, carefully placing her on the concrete front stoop, in full sunlight, where she slid off his back. The street smelled raw and stale, like it always did. Weeds grew from the washed-up silt between the curb and the street. The riverbank. There was a steady undercurrent of noise, the hum of the city. Cars and radios and people chattering and yelling, all mixing together with the choking heat, all stirring together in a stew beneath the smell of charred buildings that drifted to them from blocks away in the summer air.

"It's beautiful out," she said.

He saw the stew; he lived in it every day, but to her it was something new, different. Something beautiful.

The sun splayed across Sharon's face, and she closed her eyes and looked up at it to get its full effect. It gave Trigger a full look at her in detail, without the cover of the shadows of the house. Her hair was such a dull brown it was almost gray, the outer layer frizzed and tangled, not as straight as he'd thought. She was terribly white, almost translucent. The blue veins beneath her skin traversed their way around the black scabs on her arms, like roads carving their way around boulders. Her nails were ragged and yellow on the end, and the bags beneath her tired eyes were so brown they were the darkest thing on her. When she spoke, it seemed an effort for her to push the words out. Her teeth were small, gray and brown on the perimeter soaking into the off-white center, pale against bright pink gums. Her mouth was dry enough that her lips would get stuck on her teeth when she spoke. She had bad breath, bad enough that he had to pull back when she talked to him, like when he got too close to the camel that takes kids on rides at the zoo.

She talked about the buildings in front of them, and the bricks, and the cars on the street. How nice it all was, and how lucky they were to be there, sitting on that concrete block looking at it all. And how good the warm sun felt. It felt hot to Trigger. It looked ugly to him, and he told her. They talked incessantly, but neither really listened to the other. It seemed they were constantly on the brink of an argument, but they didn't stop talking and he didn't care about anything else. He didn't even care about whatever it was they were going on about, but it began to turn into an argument he was compelled to win, her views on their surroundings versus his. He was locked into her sickly face and her jittery hands, hands that scratched and fluttered around and pointed. He pointed back, making statements from only his perspective and getting defensive because she couldn't see things his way. He probably could have sat there blathering on about nothing until the sun expired. As he went on, Sharon's attention was drawn across the street. On the porch, with her watering can, was the old woman with the cat eyeglasses. She smiled, waving to them with her free hand.

"Helloooo!" She called to them, her voice thin but cheery.

Sharon gave a huge wave back, bending her forearm over her head, as if flagging down a ship, thrilled to have a new person in her life even just for that brief moment. Trigger looked over at the woman, then at his hand.

Just as he was ready to lift his hand, he saw it: that red, yellow, green, and black rastacap, bobbing up and down as it drifted past the homes on the other side of the street. Behind the parked cars it looked like it was floating with no body attached, like it was its own animal. A rainbow jellyfish with those dreadlocks as tentacles, riding the waves as he walked, the Rasta's dark skin blending into the shadows of the city. He coasted effortlessly with the current of the street, using it to take him where he wanted.

Trigger rose, wandering toward him, while Sharon kept talking at the sidewalk. Without realizing it, he found himself walking after the Rasta, pulled against his will like the river of lost souls that wandered the burnt-out rubble of Osage Avenue. Perhaps driven by the meth, Trigger had something he wanted to ask him, *needed* to ask him, but he struggled to remember what it was. It was something about asking forgiveness. Something to do with the zoo animals. Something about Sharon in that chair. In that room, with Bob. For not doing his part, like the Rasta was. It was an idea that faded from his mind with each step he took; soon he no longer even remembered why he needed to talk to him at all. It didn't matter. The only thing in the whole universe that mattered at that moment was that Trigger caught up to him.

By the time they'd both made it to Osage Avenue, the man had put some distance between them. Trigger's legs felt heavy, and he strained to keep up. The Rasta crossed over to the side where the yellow tape hung in front of the charred remains. The dead side. Trigger crossed too, not bothering to look for cars that might run him down. When the man turned the corner, Trigger was only halfway down the block, right in front of the MOVE house, where it all started. Trigger's pace slowed as he looked once more into what remained of that house, like he was getting close to a magnet that pulled him in, into the black past of the building.

A steel pipe reached out of the ashes, just on the other side of the tape. He came to a full stop and reached under the tape, working the pipe free from the pile of debris, rocking it back and forth. Once it broke out, he scraped at the ash with it, moving surviving bits of metal and what little wood was left. Scraping, digging. A new meth-driven obsession.

Before he realized it, he was beyond the tape, deep in the belly of the house. A single life within the entire square block, digging into the dust and choking on the fine powder that he stirred into the air. Jamming that pipe with both hands into the ground. The sweat rolling from his head, he wiped it with the back of his blackened wrist, smearing the charred remains of the dead across his face. He was determined, focused on something he didn't even understand and looking for something that he couldn't even identify, something that perhaps wasn't even there. The rainbow jellyfish, so important just a few minutes prior, totally evaporated from his thoughts as he focused on this new obsession. He rammed that pipe into the earth over and over, to the point where liquid-filled blisters rose and popped on his soft palms.

By the time a woman across the street yelled out her door for him to get out of there, he had made a crater in the ash two feet around and a foot deep. He was breathing so hard and his heart hammered so fast that he was drawing in deep lungfuls of the burned children and still didn't even understand why. He dropped the pipe and dragged himself out of the pit. His thirst raged, and the ash clung to the roof of his mouth. He shambled down the street, covered in ash and wet with sweat, looking worse than the typical dead of the neighborhood. Still high, his head floated in a bubble where only his thoughts mattered.

Numb legs drove him to the library, even the act of walking beyond his own control. The library was near empty, and the librarian at the desk watched him intensely as he crossed to the water fountain. She recognized him but stood ready to sweep him out the door if he caused an issue. He drank from the fountain until the taste of dead bodies had gone. The cool water and brisk air inside gave him new energy, and he was ready to go back outside, find another mission, but a book caught his attention, then another, then another. By the time he left the library, the heat of the day was waning and, even though it was still light out, the sun was less potent than earlier.

When he finally made it back to the house, the high from the meth had begun to dissipate, and reality started to wash back over him. He had left Sharon on the stoop with no way for her to get inside, probably for hours, and he hadn't gone to work or even called Smiley. The fear swelled and he wanted to just forget about everything again, like he had just done for this one day.

The concrete stoop was empty. The lock on the basement door was off so he assumed Bob was down there. Trigger creaked his way up the stairs as quietly as he could and saw Sharon in her chair, holding the hamster and rubbing its soft fur against her pale face. He told her how sorry he was.

"It's fine," she said. "Bob carried me up."

She slipped the hamster back into the cage and fanned herself with one of the thin books Trigger had brought her the other day.

"But," she continued, "you might not want to be around tonight. He seemed pretty pissed off."

"He's pissed? What about us? What about you? Aren't you pissed? I don't give a shit if he's pissed or not. I'm pissed."

She turned her chair toward him. Her nose and forehead had gotten sun, fading pink against that white face, color from a sun she had been watching only from behind a window for too long. She rolled to him and took his hand in hers. It was so bony and light, her skin so thin.

"You didn't think about anything, did you? Didn't feel anything? Any of the problems you're always worried about?"

Standing there, covered in ash and filth, he only shook his head to say no.

"Now you know," she said. "I don't like thinking about those problems either."

It was a risk, but he had to try for a quick shower and a change of clothes before he left. The longer he stayed, the more chance Bob would get to him, though maybe Trigger wanted him to. Maybe he wanted to just get it over with. Sometimes the fear is worse than the reality. Maybe Bob knew this and was just stalking him, playing with him and enjoying it, like a cat with a cornered mouse. Punishing him twice over. Letting his stomach wrench with possibilities and worst-case scenarios. A feeling everyone has been through, like carrying a lie that you are positive will soon be exposed. Do you act first and confess, or hope that maybe, somehow, it will get overlooked and the storm will pass quietly? Sometimes maybe the hope of a pardon makes the fall back to Earth that much worse.

He dropped his sooty clothes in a pile on the floor of his room and grabbed a crusty towel that was lying around. The shower was quick and cold. No soap or shampoo, but he dragged his fingernails across his wet scalp and it felt good. The water, gray with ash and death, ran down the stained white porcelain into the chrome drain.

He stepped lightly down the hall back to his room, clamping the towel around his pointy hips and leaving wet footprints. He shut the new bedroom door behind him, and just as he did, a thick hand wrapped around his throat, pushing his wet naked body against the peeling paint of that door. Bob was in Trigger's room waiting for him, an ambush predator, an animal that waits for the prey to come to it rather than exerting energy and hunting it down.

Bob leaned into Trigger, the key tangled in his naked hairy chest, like a thin silver egg in a black and gray bird's nest, swinging forward into Trigger's bony ribcage. Trigger tried to peel his wrist off with only his left hand, his right holding the towel, but it was firm and thick on his throat, and his hand was still wet. It slipped off. He had to drop the towel to use both hands. He stood there, wet and naked, pinned against the door and scratching at Bob's arm, gasping for breath with his father choking the air out of him. Bob's hand was so strong and solid, Trigger was at his mercy. The man was possessed, his eyes burning right through Trigger's, as red and angry as the Rasta outside the zoo, piercing into his brain.

Bob gritted his teeth, and Trigger could smell the rot, like the smell of a dead mouse in the wall. "Stop testing me," he said through clenched teeth. "Stop getting involved."

Bob slammed the back of Trigger's head against the door and released his grip. Trigger slumped to the floor, rubbing his neck and sucking in the stale hot air of the room. Bob stood looming over him, and he felt like Sharon must have felt a thousand times. Bob's hair was like a wire brush, sticking out in every direction. His eyes burned right into Trigger's, and Trigger felt as though he were about to burst into flames from that stare.

Wet and naked, sitting on that floor, he'd had enough. He was getting up to take him on. At fourteen, he was going to stand up and take his chances against his father, one naked animal to another, one generation to another. The young lion testing the older lion for control of the pride.

"Big Bob!" A voice called from downstairs. The voice snapped Bob's fixation with Trigger, and he actually shook his head to refocus. He pulled the door hard, ramming it into Trigger's back twice and forcing him to scurry out of the way.

Once Bob was in the hall, Trigger pushed the door shut and held his weight against it in case Bob tried to come back, but he didn't. Then Trigger got dressed quickly and loaded up his backpack. Creeping into the hallway, he could hear Bob talking downstairs and Trigger wanted to stay clear until he was gone. He could see Sharon's empty wheelchair in her room and a single white foot hanging off her bed.

After a few minutes, another voice entered the house, and Trigger had a feeling they weren't going anywhere anytime soon, so he went back to his room and wrapped his head in a shirt and laid on the mattress. No showdown. No fight for the pride. Just him with his head wrapped in a T-shirt, hiding in his room.

He didn't sleep, he just lay there hearing the grunts and foggy chatter and knowing Sharon heard them too. He hoped to just fall asleep, but he couldn't. Instead of cooling off after the confrontation with Bob, he became angrier with every laugh, snort, and shout he heard from downstairs. They kept him awake. They kept Sharon awake with their selfish and obnoxious behavior. He listened for close to a half hour. So tired. It was more than he could stand. He got up, angry that they wouldn't let him sleep. Angry that they were in his house, on his couch. He went to leave.

Down the stairs, Bob, one of the dead, and one of the well-dressed men from the other night sat on the couch. The well-dressed man had a bag of crystals in his lap, and he held a single large crystal between his thumb and finger, twisting it around to inspect it from all angles in the dull light. Trigger walked right by, invisible to them, Bob looking at the man's face and not paying Trigger a second of attention, almost as if he didn't even know who Trigger was.

❧

By the time Trigger got to the 34th Street bridge, it was dark out. Looking across the bridge toward the zoo, the moon leaned over his shoulder, and the lights from the bridge cascaded onto the train tracks below. Just across the bridge was Zoological Drive and the fence he would soon crawl under to get into the zoo. Zoological Drive was an elevated road that ran parallel to the train tracks, supported by pillars that held up the road and created concrete caves beneath. These were wallpapered in graffiti, each tag laying claim to the space. Trigger saw a small light, like a tiny campfire, beneath the road in the dry, protected space next to the tracks. Someone was in there.

The shower had worn off and he was sweating again. He wanted to spend the night in the bird sanctuary, but getting caught by the guard had left him spooked. He skulked through the zoo, living in the shadows of the animals, and made his way to the petting zoo, not stopping for food. Even though he hadn't eaten all day, he didn't feel hungry; he was still jittery with adrenaline. And he knew if he was caught by that guard again, it would be tough to talk his way out.

The petting zoo had sheep and goats and other small animals, and lots of hay and corners and dark places where he could stay invisible. There was a small three-sided red shed where the goats usually stayed. The hay was stacked deep in one corner, and he laid down, curling up like a dog. The rich, familiar smell of his animal past. Backpack pillow. He may have slept, but it was a sleep where he dreamed he was awake in the same place where he was. A dream uncomfortable and inescapable. The fitful sleep of a cluttered mind.

When the sun began to rise over the zoo, Trigger shook off the hay and cleaned up in a nearby bathroom, then went to the bushes near the service entrance gate, waiting for workers to file in so he could mix in with them. So tired.

He stayed in the bushes longer than he should have, making him late. He didn't want to face down Smiley. He checked his watch and let it tick past the time he was supposed to be in, holding out as long as he could take it. He gathered his nerve and went to Smiley's office. Smiley had already sent out the other workers with their assignments for the day. When Trigger pushed the door to the office open, Smiley was standing, back to the door, staring at a map of the zoo. He looked over his shoulder, then back to the wall. Trigger took a deep breath through his nose and blew it out.

"About yesterday," Trigger said. "I'm really sorry."

Smiley's head nodded on that thin neck without looking back.

"Things happened that I couldn't do anything about."

"I guess nobody could," Smiley replied.

Smiley turned around and sat in his chair, leaning back and locking his long fingers behind his head. He didn't smile. In fact, it might have been the saddest Trigger had ever seen him.

"It won't happen again," Trigger promised.

"How can you make that promise?"

He didn't know the answer. He ran his hand through his thin blonde hair and pulled back a piece of hay from the night before.

"It won't. I won't do it again, I promise."

"Won't do what? Watchu talking about?"

Trigger waited, not knowing exactly what Smiley meant, figuring he would see if he went on. He did.

"We have to clean it out now. I want it all outta there, this morning."

Trigger shook his head and raised his shoulders in question.

"The prairie dog," Smiley finally said. "The prairie dog we made up the pen for."

Trigger hunched his shoulders again. "You want to move it out of there?"

Smiley tipped his chair forward and dragged his hands across his dark face, rubbing his palms, scuffed and tough as a baseball hide, into his closed eyes, then covered his face.

"The prairie dog," he muttered through his hands. "It died yesterday. It died givin' birth. Two of the three pups died too, and without the mamma, that last one gonna die sure enough."

Trigger slumped into the chair in front of his desk, dropping the backpack onto the floor. Smiley wasn't accusing him, wasn't talking about Trigger's yesterday. His jaw opened to say something, but not a breath left his mouth.

Smiley shook his head, his shoulders slumping, then slapped his palms on the desk.

"The vet took that baby, but ain't no way it's gonna make it without its mamma." He clucked his tongue in his cheek, and a crooked, sad grin spread across his dark face. "Take a few cans up there and a rake. Get all that hay outta there and clean it up. Take the hay over to the storage shed for now."

Trigger picked up his pack to leave.

"And meet me for lunch, eleven-thirty, at the bench."

The door where the security guard had caught Trigger was open, and he dragged a large plastic trash can down the hall and into the pen. It was empty but still smelled like the prairie dog, a musty smell mixed from animal and hay and captivity. There was a hole where it had burrowed, and the hay was still flat where Trigger had lain with it. He peeked down the corridor both ways, making sure he was alone, then entered the pen. He sat cross-legged in the hay, right where the prairie dog had been. Then he laid down. He curled up, took in its scent, and closed his eyes, picturing how peaceful it had been when they were both there, together, and how safe and warm he had felt. Then his chin started to quiver, and the tears came close to squeezing from the corners of his eyes.

He got up and pinched at the bridge of his nose, forcing the tears back. Brushing the hay from his clothes, he shook off the memory of the prairie dog. It took three cans to get all the hay up.

After he'd swept it out clean, he just stood there, looking into the empty pen, the same as if he were back on that cold concrete stoop staring into the burnt-out lot of the MOVE house.

He dropped the hay off at the shed, took a pan and broom, and wandered the zoo for trash, even though Smiley hadn't told him to. He made his way to the bird sanctuary, sweeping up bits of garbage here and there, a thoughtless job that normally allowed his mind to roam somewhere else, but all he could think about was where he was.

In the sanctuary, Trigger stopped at the bridge to listen to the water, the same bridge he liked to sleep under. The water collected in a small, quiet, still pool on the other side of the bridge where it filtered through the system again. A small ring of ripples caught his eye, and he climbed over the wood rail to see. In the pool was a bee, struggling in the water. Its wings were wet and heavy, and it was just a matter of time before its energy was spent and it drowned. It was just a bee, but it was suffering, fighting with all it had to survive. He reached the broom handle into the water, giving it a lifeline. It clung on, and he lifted it out of the pond. It spread its shear wings out to dry, and he gently tapped it off the broom onto the wood rail by the bridge and climbed back through. He backed out, watching it walk on the rail while waiting for its wings to dry. It took off but was still too heavy with water, and it landed on the wooden walking path that cut through the sanctuary. No sooner had it landed when a family of four, two young parents with two small girls in white dresses, shiny white shoes, and pink headbands, crossed that bridge. The younger of the two girls, maybe five or six, saw that bee. She pointed it out to her older sister, saying "A bee!" and stomped down into the deck, mashing the bee between wood and rubber. That bee, for all its struggle and effort, for all its panic of drowning and of working to save its small life, was crushed so easily into the wood plank. That bee, just pulled back from another certain death, couldn't escape its fate. Trigger watched it happen and couldn't understand the point of it all.

When they walked off, he swept the bee back into the water, where he felt he should have left it in the first place.

# Eleven

For a few days after he smoked the meth, Trigger slept at the zoo and didn't go to the house at all. He got cleaned up in the bathrooms and ate from the snack shack, taking just enough food from the supply closet that it was unlikely to be missed, and spent the nights with his animal family. After that, he went back to the house during the day to feel things out.

When he got there, the basement door was padlocked, but Bob wasn't home, which seemed unusual. Sharon told him Bob had left the day before but hadn't told her where he was going. He had left her food and water in the bedroom, along with a fat bag of crystals. If Trigger had known, he would have been there with her. That night he stayed in her room and helped her study, questioning her and reading from the books he had brought. She tried her best and, for one rare moment, the promise of a better future motivated her.

She squinted and wrestled with words, but after a while her dyslexia won out and she gave up and hit the pipe, pulling in the smoke, her face sucking in tight and looking like a thin sheet of white plastic drawn over bones. It was late into the night when he couldn't fight off sleep anymore. He got up to go to his room.

"Sleep in here tonight?" she asked. "I don't want to be alone again."

Her eyes were red and glassy, and she struggled to keep them open, pleading with him through the thin slits from which she witnessed her world. He looked at that bed, those sheets, and saw Bob and her tangled together. When he told her no, she asked to sleep in his room with him. He agreed and bent down for her to climb onto his back.

"I want to do it myself."

She tried her best to squeeze her old wheelchair through that door frame, but Bob made sure it wouldn't fit.

"Go find a hammer or something. Take that wood off so I can get out of here on my own."

Trigger rummaged around the clutter in the dark kitchen, then on the rear porch, stumbling around until he found a thick flat screwdriver. So tired, always tired. No hammer found, he brought a heavy flat rock from the yard as well. He smacked the screwdriver between that trim and the door frame, prying and twisting. It creaked with strain and slowly gave way. Bits of wood broke off, but the nails stayed in place, sticking out of the frame like steel ribs. He managed to get enough of the trim off and some nails bent back so that Sharon was able to roll out of the room for the first time in what seemed an eternity.

She stopped in the hallway and looked down the stairs into the living room below, that other world, then went into his room, what used to be their room. She looked around and stopped in the doorway, leaving him in the hall. There were still a few things of hers in there, things belonging to the girl that used to sleep there. Another girl she no longer was. Beside the window was a green stuffed monkey. He had seen her sleep with it almost every night when they shared the room. She went to it, struggling to roll over some clothes, a few soda bottles, and towels piled on the floor. She picked up the stuffed toy and brushed it off, rubbing it against her face.

Her bed had been removed, and there was just the one mattress on the floor now. Trigger helped her to it, and he laid on the floor beside the mattress.

"No, on here," she said.

He worked his way onto the mattress, his back to her chest. She draped her left arm over him and pulled herself in close, her bra-less chest pressed against his back. She hummed and played with his hair with her other hand. Trigger's breath became quick, and all of a sudden he wasn't so tired anymore. Her lips were close to his ear, and she hummed a type of lullaby, a lullaby that he remembered his mother singing to her but not to him. Her lips brushed his skin until the hot words dripped into his ear.

"I have a dog that likes to roam . . . he tries to find a better home . . . I have a rabbit who runs from his pen, when he gets out . . . I put him back in . . . I have a bird that doesn't fly . . . afraid she'll get lost in the endless sky . . ."

She spoke the words so softly and pushed her body into his so tightly that all he could do was clamp his eyes shut. His body was rigid, and she had to have sensed it. It was confusing and a little frightening to him, as he had never been that close to a girl, or any type of a woman, before. His penis stiffened, pushing against his jeans and bent the wrong way, but he couldn't move to adjust it. All he wanted was to fall asleep, or have her fall asleep, but neither of them could. That song in his ear, the song of his mother played over and over. Eventually, probably near morning, he drifted off.

❧

There was the collision, and he was covered with that shattered glass, showering over them. The screaming and the twisting of steel groaning, and the fire.

❧

Rabbit rabbit.

The creaking of the steps. The sun pouring through the brown stained windows of the room, trapping in the heat. Sharon and Trigger had both turned over, and now his chest was to her back, and he was shaped to her, pressing into her warm body from behind. His penis was still hard, but it was also cold and wet. His clothes were on, as hers were, but he had ejaculated in his pants while he'd slept. He lifted his arm from her as silently as he could to roll off the bed without waking her, and as he did, there was Bob.

"What in the fuck is going on here?"

Bob stood in the doorway, digesting what he saw at his feet, and each passing second must have forced his paranoid mind further and further toward suggesting the unthinkable. He stood there fully clothed, not shirtless as usual, and it looked unnatural, like a circus monkey wearing jeans and a shirt. As Trigger went to stand, Bob hit him, full fist, right in the eye socket, rocking him back so that he fell across the mattress and onto Sharon. He rarely struck Trigger with a closed fist, and that fist of stone landed solid, sending a white flash through Trigger's brain. He was helpless and expected Bob to pounce, but he didn't.

Trigger shook it off and rolled from Sharon onto the floor, covering up and trying to get back to the world. Bob straddled over him and reached down with both hands, lifting him off the floor by the back of his jeans and his shirt collar, cutting into his neck. He threw Trigger across the tiny room, and he landed in a tangled heap onto the wheelchair, then crumpled to the floor. Sharon was up and pleading with Bob that she was afraid to sleep alone, it was her fault, and that she heard someone downstairs the night before looking for him. Trigger was able to get to his feet when Bob came at him again. This time he was able to block his powerful right with an arm, but it was still enough to knock him back into the chair again. Bob cocked once more, and without even thinking, Trigger kicked him, right in the balls. It wasn't a direct shot, but it was enough to give his father a jolt and stop the assault. Bob bent over, hands on his knees, and caught his breath. Right there, while he was bent over and struggling to breathe, Trigger had the chance to kick him right in the face. It would have done damage, Bob would have felt it for sure, he would have known he was there. Trigger tensed up and balled his fists in preparation, but Sharon snapped her fingers and pointed frantically to the wheelchair, lips tight and eyes large. Trigger lost his edge and pushed it to her, and she got in. She looked at Bob and rubbed his back while he stayed bent over.

"He was just looking out for me," she said, massaging the fur beneath his shirt but looking right into Trigger's eyes.

Bob shook it off and pushed Sharon out of the room.

"I'll deal with you later," he said to Trigger.

Bob slammed the door behind them as they went to their side of the house.

"I'll deal with you now," he heard Bob say to Sharon in the hall.

"This isn't right!" Trigger shouted. "You can't treat people like this!"

He kicked at the clothes on the floor, and from some corner of darkness in him he remembered something that touched him somehow, and he shouted it out. "Fuck this system!"

He changed out of his sticky pants and underwear as quickly as he could and left. No backpack, no money, no anything. A big maroon van sat parked on the street outside the house, one Trigger had never seen before. Most of the cars were the same ones all the time, in the same spots, as neighbors respected each other's claimed parking spaces in the street. His eye was pulsing. The blood rushed to it, making it hot and sensitive, and he wanted something cool to put on it, but there was nothing but heat outside. He had been awake less than half an hour and was already so bitter and pissed off, he could only wonder how things were going to get worse as the day ground on.

The answer got to him before he made it to the end of the block. Turning the corner just ten feet from him was Will Thomas, heading right at him. Trigger paused and took in a deep breath, rubbing at the eye with the back of his hand, just waiting for Will to start in on him like he always did, relentlessly poking Trigger just for the sake of poking at him.

"Hey! Nee-Gro! Whatchu doing boy? You wanna give it a go?"

He jammed that shoulder into Trigger and jumped a half step back, throwing up his fists. Trigger tensed his hands by his ears, fingers stretched out and screaming into the sidewalk.

"Jesus! What is wrong with you? All of you! This whole fucking city! What is wrong with you?"

Will stopped dancing. "I know you ain't talking that way to me, is you?" He stepped in again, and again jammed that tight shoulder into Trigger's.

Without thinking, Trigger shoved both his palms into Will's chest, knocking him back into a concrete stoop. Will lost his balance and stumbled into a seated position on the steps. Trigger stormed off, staring right into the cracked sidewalk and shouting furiously to himself, just like the insane people he saw every day on those streets who were alone and screaming about the world, about their problems, to no one. He didn't look back at Will, whom Trigger thought he heard yelling something about how he was going to kick some ass but had someplace to be or something. Trigger didn't even care, and Will didn't follow him.

He'd left the house in such a rush he hadn't even put shoes on and so had to step lightly to avoid the glass and pebbles threatening his bare feet. He walked with his head down, focused only on the sidewalk and his aggravation, not looking up. People out starting their day stepped out of his path, just the way he would get out of the way of a barefoot derelict pacing the street. A boy about his age, with an afro like Troy Thomas's, bounced a basketball on the sidewalk, his eyes nervously glued to the ball while trying to avoid contact with Trigger's.

Trigger's feet toughened against the hot concrete. The damp smell of ash drew him toward Osage Avenue.

He needed his backpack and shoes and some other things if he was going to spend most of the day out. After about an hour of stomping the streets and cursing to himself like the insane dead do, he went back to the house, feet red with the heat of the city and his eye closing up. The van was gone and so was Bob. Sharon said Bob had just bought it and had gone with Will somewhere, which aggravated Trigger even more. She was holding the hamster and staring out the fogged window. He looked around her room with one eye. Something was missing.

"Where are the books?"

She took a deep breath in, then exhaled. "Bob took them," she said matter-of-factly.

"Took them? Took them where?"

She shrugged, just petting the fur as its small heart quickly pulsed in her hands.

He looked around the living room and even wasted time pulling on the padlocked basement door to see if he could get it open. He found the books in a pile of smoldering ash in the small concrete backyard. The interior pages of some of the thicker books were still intact, protected by the heavy bindings and the outer pages that were sacrificed, but the majority were burned up. Gone. He picked up a stick, squatted down, and poked at it. Some light black ash rose and drifted, falling only a few feet from where they had begun. The lighter white ash in the center still had a few glowing embers on it, and the papers fused together, waiting to slowly turn to nothingness. He sat there and watched those embers until they burned out, leaving just ash, like on Osage Avenue.

When he went back upstairs, Sharon had her pipe out and sparked it just as he entered the room. She held it out to him as she held her own hit in. He studied her face while she struggled to hold that smoke in and was disgusted. He couldn't help it. He hated it, and he hated her for offering it to him. But he understood. She was just a scared kid too. Even though she was a few years older, in many ways he knew much more of the world than she did, and maybe she just wanted someone to be in *her* world for a little while, the only world she knew, with her.

He hit the pipe, drawing in and getting back on that roller coaster. They smoked and she talked. She went on about random things, things she knew nothing about. About the hamster, and if she were to let it go free, how it would never be able to survive because all that it knew was its cage. About the MOVE people, and why the loudspeakers had screamed across the neighborhood, and why the city burnt their house down. About the universe, about living and dying and the afterlife. About everything and nothing, and she spoke like an expert on it all, scattering her thoughts and ideas around like seeds on fresh soil. And the more she went on, the more Trigger wanted to call her out. He started to argue with her about those things, things that neither of them knew anything about.

Trigger hadn't eaten, and before he smoked he was feeling hungry, but that went away. Everything went away. He walked back outside, down the street, then back to the house and smoked more. He sat in the yard and poked at the dead ash of the books, as if he were poking at the dead of Osage Avenue. When he became bored with that, he meandered back inside, stopping to tug at the padlock on the basement door. He had a craving, one like he'd never felt before, and it pulled him back to Sharon's room, just like the street dead were pulled into the house. Sharon had another pipe and gave it to him, along with a lighter and a small bag of crystals. It got dark, and he sat on the couch and smoked by himself, just staring at the wall in front of him. At some point Bob came home, but Trigger had no idea what time it was. Bob looked at him on that couch and just smiled, and Trigger smiled back. They both smiled for different reasons, neither of them good.

❧

He fell asleep, and the grill of that truck woke him up, smashing into them and spraying glass into his hair and trying to cook them alive, forcing him back into the world he was trying to escape.

❧

He smoked more. He forgot more. He cared less. He smoked to the point where he ran out.

The basement door was unlocked, and Trigger drifted over to it, almost beyond his power to stop the movement even if he wanted to. Swinging the door open, the fumes hit him, and he realized that he had been sitting in a thinner smog from those fumes the whole time—he had just gotten used to it. Floating down the steps, it was brighter than he imagined down there, and Bob was shirtless with a black respirator strapped across his face, moving and pouring and measuring, pulling the mask off and snorting, then back on to work more. There were tubes and liquids, cleaning fluid and propane. Open flames and all kinds of bottles, like the lab from an old horror movie where the demented doctor created life where it shouldn't have been created. Trigger stumbled toward it like a zombie summoned by its master.

Muffled by the respirator, Bob cursed and screamed through it at him, but the words dissipated into the smog. Bob pointed at the door and Trigger left, shutting it behind him, unfazed. He shambled into the kitchen and found a bag of some kind of chips and ate them, then drank water from the sink. He pushed a pile of dishes out of the way, and one of them slipped out and crashed to the floor. He didn't care. Nobody cared. He stuck his head under that faucet, hair lying in the filth of those dishes, and slurped like he had been wandering a desert for weeks. Upstairs he pestered Sharon for more, begging as he had seen the desperate dead do so many times. So many times he had been disgusted by them. But now she was less generous and more defensive, though she did give up some. When he went to take a leak in the bathroom, he saw in the cracked mirror that his left eye was as purple and black as a plum and almost entirely closed.

Back to the couch, that safe couch. It was comfortable. It was familiar and he didn't want to move from it and he started to understand why people were always on it. Not a lot could go wrong if you just stayed on that couch. Later on a few people came to the house, and one sat on the other end of the couch while one went to the basement. The man smoked, then Trigger smoked. He talked, then Trigger talked, then neither of them talked. Trigger looked at him, and he looked right back at Trigger, like a filthy mirror, and there he was, one of the dead he had always feared he would become.

For the next few days, it went like that, in and out of two realities but slowly fading into just one. Sometimes the heat in the house made his back wet with sweat against the couch, sometimes he didn't feel it.

It was the most Trigger could remember getting along with Bob; even though Bob was constantly yelling at him, it didn't penetrate like it used to. It bounced off. An invisible bubble, just like the people outside the zoo ignoring the bullhorn. Trigger really didn't care if Bob yelled or not, or if he was there or not, or really about anything, and that felt good enough. People drifted in and floated out with the tide of the river, and Sharon was less important, dealing with her own world in her own room. Even Will Thomas came in once and Trigger felt nothing toward him as Will laughed at him and jabbed at the air. He just stayed glued to that couch, Velcro growing out of his back and into those cushions, and it was fine. Everything stable. No future, and he couldn't see the past through the cloud of smoke. Osage Avenue was ten thousand miles away.

Then there was a knock.

People didn't knock on the door, they just came in.

It started with short, sharp clicks on the door, like one knuckle tapping. Trigger didn't move. The knuckle became the meaty part of a fist, making a dull fat thud. It wouldn't stop, and if he didn't peel himself off that Velcro, that thud would have pounded on him forever, banging into his brain and not letting him rot in peace.

By the time he made it to the door, Bob had come up the stairs from his cave, and just as he was dead-bolting that basement door, just as the word "DON'T!" left his mouth, Trigger pulled that front door open and the banging stopped.

The summer sunlight poured into the house, reminding him that the outside world continued on without him, and he drew back like a vampire. In the doorway were a set of clothes hanging off a stick figure. Tall and dark, relaxed enough to have his arm leaning against the door frame.

Smiley took off his gray zoo hat and bent just enough so his head and torso peeked into the house, his grin reaching to his back teeth. "So," he said. "You still alive."

Trigger opened the door wider and Smiley stepped in. The light from outside splayed across that dank living room, it shone across the floor, climbing up the walls and onto Bob, who squinted into it just like Trigger did with his one good eye. Smiley came in and Trigger closed the door behind him, shutting out that other reality.

Bob didn't step closer. Shirtless and shoeless, his wild frazzled hair spiking out in all directions, he stood silent. He had red strap marks across his face from the respirator. Smiley took two long strides across the room and nodded at Bob, hat in hand and stretched out his long arm, that wide, leathery palm searching for Bob's hand.

"Hey, I'm Sam . . . Trey's boss. Sam?"

He stood there, bent over, hand out and a smile peeled across his face, waiting for Bob to lift his arm. He didn't. Bob stood bolted to the floor, leery and judging.

"What d'you want?" was all he said.

Smiley pulled back, slipped his hat back on, hooked his thumbs into the belt loops of his pants, and chuckled.

"I came looking for Trey. Hasn't been to work in a few days. No phone call, no nothing. No phone number in his file, just this here address. Just making sure he's all right." Smiley might have sneaked a look up at Trigger's still partly closed eye, but if he did, Trigger didn't notice, wasn't paying attention.

Bob squinted and scratched the stubble on his cheek with long fingernails. "File? What file you got on him?"

There came creaking from the hardwood upstairs, and Trigger

turned his head just enough to see Sharon rolling from her bedroom to the top of the stairs, looking down at them.

"*Work* file." Smiley said, hitting the word *work* hard. "You know, work. A file for people at work." Smiley, though speaking, ignored Bob and looked Trigger up and down, and now Trigger's one good eye followed Smiley's gaze.

Then Trigger looked to the floor, realizing for the first time he had never even put on shoes that morning, days earlier, when he had run out of the house, and that had been the main reason he had come back, to put shoes on, and he never had. He hadn't changed clothes either, or washed himself or brushed his teeth or done really anything. He pretty much hadn't moved in days, and seeing Smiley there in his work clothes, clean and alive, gave him such a feeling of shame and embarrassment he wanted to just drift away like a speck of ash, invisible in the darkness. Like he had been. Numb.

"You okay?" Smiley asked.

Trigger knew how he looked. He had seen it on dozens of the drugged dead of the neighborhood. The swelling had gone down some in his eye, but it was still as dark as Smiley's skin.

"He's fine." Bob barked.

"Uhh huhh . . . Don't look too fine to me," Smiley replied. Smiley leaned in closer, so Bob couldn't hear, and tilted his head, squinting one eye at Trigger, whispering, "Is that right? You fine son?"

He nodded yes.

"Good. Then go get changed. We got work to do. You know . . ." he looked again toward Bob, "*work*?"

"What'r you trying to say?" Bob ripped his roots free of the wood floor and stepped closer. Smiley didn't move an inch back and kept looking right into Bob's pocked face.

"I'm saying the boy got responsibilities. He's got a job to do, and I'm gonna make sure he gets to it."

"He don't gotta go nowhere. And he don't gotta listen to no coon neither. Sit down, Trigger, sit down and stay."

Smiley turned his lips in and cocked his neck side to side, like a boxer at the stare-down before a fight. He balled up his fists for just a second, then took a deep breath in through his wide flat nose and let it out through his mouth, relaxing his hands. He nodded his head and laughed, letting out all the anger. He smiled again at Trigger, those white straight teeth floating in the darkness. "Let's go."

Trigger looked at Bob in the shadows, then up at Sharon, her chair still at the top of the steps.

"You should go," she said, then she pulled back, clearing a path to his room.

He felt the gritty hardwood beneath his bare feet and the throbbing in his eye, like the blood was starting to slowly move through his body again. It seemed to take all his strength to get up those stairs.

Halfway up he turned back to look at both Smiley and Bob. Black and white. The duality of the universe. Both standing in the darkness of that room, both with their own agendas and issues. Both with a past that had led them to where they were right then, right in that room looking up at him, waiting for him to decide his own future.

In the hall, with Bob and Smiley beneath them looking up, Sharon grabbed Trigger's arm as he passed and pulled him in.

She whispered just loud enough for him to hear. "Don't come back."

He packed up some clothes, leaving the stained underwear from the other night on the floor. He heard the front door close, and after he got dressed, he looked down the stairs and saw that Smiley was gone. Trigger went to the bathroom, and as he rinsed his face in the sink, he looked into the mirror and saw that eye, and behind him

Sharon. He dried off his face on the sleeves of his shirt and turned to her.

"I'll be back after work. I'm not going anywhere without you."

She shook her head. "That's never gonna happen."

He went down the stairs as the lighter flickered in her room.

Trigger pulled the front door open and the summer poured in, exposing millions of dust motes whipping around in the sunlight, stirred up by the motion. Millions of swirling galaxies that no one would ever notice and that would make no difference when they disappeared forever, their universe in complete upheaval with one swing of the door and a slight breeze, and they didn't even realize it.

# Twelve

THE SMOKE WAS SO THICK HE COULDN'T COME up for air. He had to hold his breath longer than he thought he could, until the pain in his chest was almost as bad as the heat reaching over the front seats to swallow him.

⁂

Rabbit rabbit.

Don't forget. Don't give up.

⁂

It was the first time he'd slept in the elephant exhibit. There were three elephants, all female. Smiley said when the oldest female in a herd died, that elephant's daughter would take over as matriarch, even if the female that died had a sister older than that daughter. The responsibility always passed down from mother to daughter, to look out for the family if the mother died.

Trigger stayed beyond the small green fence on the outside of their exhibit. There was a large moat with dark green algae and a rock wall on both sides they couldn't get over. A middle ground, where the elephants could not reach and where the public was not allowed. A few years before, when you were still permitted to toss peanuts to the elephants, kids would do their best, hoping to see one of them pick one up. Maybe it made the kids feel directly connected to the animals, like they were pets being fed, like the animals needed them, relied on them. The children inevitably tossed peanuts short of the wall and into the ravine. One female elephant kept reaching over the wall, stretching and pushing herself as far onto the wall as she could, reaching with her dexterous trunk for the unclaimed nuts. She fell in and injured her leg. It happened twice more with the same elephant, eventually leaving her somewhat crippled from the injuries. After that, the zoo banned any feeding of the elephants. When word of this hit the newspaper, the MOVE members stormed the front of the zoo every day for weeks, spitting into bullhorns, alive with anger and righteousness.

As Trigger lay there that night, crammed between a tree and fence, the elephants roamed back and forth across the dusty enclosure. He was the only one there, watching like a spy as they paced under a starless city sky. One side, then the other. One wall, then another. Smiley said that a family of elephants could move up to a hundred miles in a day. Not these elephants. The entire area was no more than a half-acre of city dirt. Maybe if they paced across a thousand times, they could reach that in a day. And maybe they did.

There were no happy kids laughing with balloons, no monorail above, no birthday parties or school trips or young parents pushing strollers. It was just him and those elephants, wondering why there was a wall and why the earth suddenly stopped, then turning back, looking for open ground only to find another wall just a few paces away. They grunted in frustration and distress, hoping their family could hear them, blowing their trumpets for help. Those trumpets could be heard for six miles in the wild, but here they were smothered by the sounds of the city. Trigger was the one human being to hear their cries of loneliness and confusion, living it with them and unable to help. Elephants can also get angry, hurting and killing people in the wild who come too close or who threaten them. Trigger imagined these elephants had every reason to be just as angry, captive as they were, angry as MOVE had been for them.

⁂

After Smiley showed up at the house, Trigger didn't go home for five nights. That first day, after Trigger walked out that door and saw Smiley sitting on the concrete stoop smoking a cigarette, out in the sunlight with his bony back to him, he just wanted to stay outside. Smiley had a tan 1966 Chevy Impala SS double-parked next to Bob's van. It was a two-door, with black leather seats and a hood that stretched out as long as the rest of the car. When Trigger sat in it, he was in another world, one that smelled like cigarettes and hot leather.

The windows were down, and Smiley adjusted the knobs on the radio with his black licorice fingertips as they drove out of West Philadelphia. Away from the burned-down MOVE house with the standing brick walls, past the Thomas brothers and Bob and the zoo. All the way to North Philadelphia, to Smiley's rowhouse. The neighborhood didn't look much better than Trigger's; in fact, in a lot of ways it looked worse. There were parked cars with flat tires, and trash in the street, and weeds working their way through the concrete sidewalks. The brick homes held in all the same heat and frustration as in Trigger's neighborhood, but there were more people on porches, more graffiti on the houses, and more houses boarded up.

There were small grass front yards, maybe ten feet by ten feet, high with weeds, caged in by bent and rusted wire fencing, like patches of wild jungle struggling to reclaim the land.

Smiley's house was dead in the middle of the street, and he pulled into a large empty parking spot right in front, like everyone knew he was coming and they'd left it for him.

Trigger took his backpack and followed Smiley up the steps. There was a group of black guys on a porch two houses down and they yelled out, "Uncle Sam!" Smiley laughed and yelled some things back to them about getting a job, then unlocked the heavy white metal screen door to get to the wood one. There was no screen left in the door, but the metal bars were thick and square, like a bank teller's cage. Another key for the front door and they were in. The door didn't creak like at Trigger's house. There was carpet, brown and green. Ugly but clean. There was a couch and table and a television. Everything was organized and where it should have been, with photos in frames on the walls, and bulbs in the light fixtures. The couch was covered in a plastic sleeve, and even though a heavy green ashtray sat on the table, the home didn't smell like smoke. It was clean enough that it almost didn't seem lived in. Sterile.

"What are we doing here?" Trigger asked.

Smiley locked the door behind them and hung the keys neatly on a small hook by the door.

"I just figured you might want to crash here for a day or so. Just to catch yo breath. I need to get you back to work is all."

The room was small but well lit, and the living room opened up right into a small kitchen with a linoleum floor. In the kitchen sat a round table in the center with two white chairs. Trigger slowly crossed the room, looking at the photos on the wall. One with a black couple, the man with dark-rimmed glasses and a wide lapel on a blue suit, and the woman in a white dress with lace. Smiley's parents. It looked old but not dusty. There was another beside that, a boy maybe six or seven, sitting in the sand with a yellow bucket and a blue ocean in the background. He was smiling, smiling right at Trigger, and Trigger locked into that smile.

"Why do you need me back?" he asked, still staring at the photo.

Smiley ignored the question.

"That's Antoine, my boy. That's him in San Diego." Smiley walked up from behind and stretched his long arm out to straighten the frame a bit. Unconsciously, he gave out a little wistful sigh. Then he turned back to Trigger.

"Nice beach there. And a really nice zoo. Second nicest zoo in America." He smiled at the picture for another second, then laid that huge hand, black as tire rubber, over Trigger's shoulder.

The Philadelphia Zoo had a great silverback gorilla. He was the leader of the whole group of gorillas. Smiley told him a group of gorillas is a troop. A troop, like in the Army. He saw that silverback once, lay its hand on one of its troop. He didn't know why, or if it was just by chance, but he felt that same presence. That same hand, dry and powerful, fingernails worn down and cracked. Each line in each knuckle powdered with age, laying on his shoulder.

"Why don't you go upstairs and get cleaned up, take a shower. Take the first room, right up top of the stairs."

The steps didn't groan, they were solid and sure. In the room was a small bed with a spread covered in Phillies logos. There were Phillies pennants on walls covered with pin-striped wallpaper, and two small trophies on the white dresser. Everything was clean and where it was supposed to be, and Trigger didn't even want to touch anything and have his filth rub off.

He dropped his backpack on the floor and peeked down the hall. The bathroom was at the end, and he went to it, leaving his clothes in a heap on the floor and running the shower. The water was warm and there was soap and shampoo. He let that warm water wash over him and shampooed over and over.

There was a light knock on the door and it opened, and Trigger could see a figure through the thin shower curtain. His heart pumped faster, eyes wide and the shampoo stinging, fixed on that figure creeping in. He should have figured it was all too perfect. Good things didn't happen to him. There was a whole world out there full of other people for good things to happen to, but not him. He had let his guard down, for just a minute, and now it was time to pay.

Smiley slipped into the steamy bathroom. Trigger pictured that tiger anticipating feeding time, pacing before its meal. He tensed up, wet, naked, and vulnerable, clutching the shampoo bottle close to his chest and holding his breath like the kids in the MOVE house must have done when the smoke swirled around them. Smiley slid silently across the room, and Trigger had no place to hide. Exposed and naked and at the world's mercy.

"Hey," Smiley said. Trigger could see his shadowy frame stooping down. "I'm just gonna wash these here clothes, okay? And the clothes in yo bag."

He scooped up the dirty, ashy clothes and Trigger let out his breath. "I left you some clean clothes on the bed," he said.

He closed the door behind him, and even though Trigger was the cleanest he had been in months, he felt more dirty and trashy than he ever had.

Smiley left a pair of shorts and a T-shirt. They were too big for Trigger, but he didn't care; they smelled like the white flowers in the bird sanctuary. His backpack was empty and on the bed too.

When he went downstairs, he saw Smiley sitting at the small kitchen table, set neat with two sets of plates and silverware. There was a bowl of pasta on the table with a little plate of bread beside it. Trigger sat, and Smiley scooped a heap of pasta with meat sauce onto his plate, then filled a large glass with milk for him. Then Smiley sat and made his own plate. As Trigger started shoveling food into his mouth, Smiley shut his eyes, bowed his head, and took the time to bless himself, his lips moving but no words leaving his mouth. Trigger stopped eating for the few seconds it took until he was done. They ate silently, not an awkward silence like the first few times they had lunch together, more of a comfortable quiet, almost proving they didn't need to speak.

Trigger's eyes drifted around the room, taking in the white ceiling and white cabinets. There were big wooden spoons on the walls and a toaster on the small counter by the sink. Smiley had a beer with his food, and he took swigs with mouthfuls of meat and pasta.

Trigger's chewing slowed, and he swallowed and cleared his throat. "Why are you doing this for me?"

Smiley looked up, those deep-set eyes squinting in thought, then took another slug of beer. Pausing for a second, he blew a deep breath out of his wide nose, then ripped off a chunk of bread with his teeth and spoke over it.

"They didn't always call me Smiley," was all he said.

Trigger considered this and twirled some pasta onto his fork, lifting it halfway to his mouth, then hesitated. He was about to let the matter slide by and take things to be just as they seemed, but he could smell the soap on his skin from the shower and felt the clean, soft fabric of the shirt, and pressed Smiley.

"I don't know what that means," he continued. "Why do you want to do this for me? The job at the zoo, this . . . all of it?"

Smiley took another deep breath and cocked his neck from side to side. He sneaked a quick glance toward the framed picture on the wall.

"Sometimes," he began, "sometimes in nature, some animals . . ." He stopped and took a long slug from his beer. "No. That ain't right. I was gonna be going off on something 'bout animals, dancing 'round the question. You old enough. You in the middle of all this. I can be straight with you. I can talk to you like a man."

He slid his beer to the side.

"When I was a kid, I had no father. Not like I was no orphan or nothing, just had a no-good kinda bum for a father who up and left when I was a good bit younger than you. My mamma did her best to raise us, but I got three other brothers and a sister, and ain't no way she could handle us and still keep a roof over our heads. I had, I guess you could say, too much freedom. Too much time off on my own. Idle hands are the devil's workshop, you know? Got me in all kinds of trouble, and by the time I was about yo age, maybe a little older, she kicked me out. Can't say I blame her. I was a bad apple, just a wannabe bad ass, a scared kid, 'bout to spoil the rest of the bunch. It took me a long time and a lotta help from some good people to set me right, and when I got a little older, I swore that if I ever had me a kid, ain't no way I was gonna fuck it up like my daddy did."

He picked up the beer, nervously tapping the bottom of the bottle on the table, as if letting out excessive energy that was building up in his system.

"Sorry for the swear word. That ain't right either. Anyway, I promised I would be there if I ever had me a kid. Doin' the right thing, you know? Well, I had me a kid. And he's all the way the hell out in California, and here I am, right here where I always been. I ain't there for him."

He took a pause and shook his head. "So much for doin' the right thing I guess."

He held the bottle to his lips and took the last sip, holding it there after that last drop of beer was well gone.

"When I seen you that time at the zoo, that time when those kids jumped you, I seen what you did. You did the right thing, sticking up for the animals, even though you was gonna get a beatin' for it. That takes courage. Those animals are innocent, and behind a fence, they couldn't defend themselves. Made me proud. Made me hope maybe my boy, Antoine, was the same way as you was. Maybe made me think that was the kind of kid I wished I'd raised. The kind of kid I wished I was when I was yo age. You got a good heart. I just don't wanna see it get too hard. I been there. Sometimes it's a long way back. Some people can't do it. Maybe you just need someone in yo life looking out for you a bit. Maybe you just need some guidance."

He stood and swiped the beer bottle off the table, turning his back to Trigger. He stopped at the sink and put the bottle on the counter, and without looking back said, "But maybe I just need someone I can look out for. Could be I'm just being selfish, making it seem like I'm doin' this for you, when I'm really doin' it for me."

He cocked his neck to both sides and blew out his nose. "I'm really hoping that's not the case."

The next day they drove to the zoo together. Smiley asked him to stay for another night or two, but Trigger said no. Smiley didn't ask again, he just nodded and smiled saying, "Just so you know, you always got a place with Uncle Sam."

Trigger didn't respond, he just stared out the windshield into the morning sun bathing the city.

Smiley continued. "What I'm saying is, if you want, if you need, you can stay with me. At my house. Yo sister too if she wants. At least until we can get you situated somewhere else. You have options, even if it don't seem like you do."

He'd spent just that one night at Smiley's before he went back to the zoo, back to the captured animals. To the elephants.

♣

When he woke up in the elephant exhibit, it was still dark. Elephants don't sleep for more than a few hours a day, just like Trigger, though they sleep more in captivity; with no natural threats, they are supposedly more relaxed. But they didn't seem relaxed. They were up, pacing and groaning before Trigger was. Dragging through the dust, pacing to one wall then back to the other, looking for the way out again and again.

After the night Trigger had stayed at Smiley's, Trigger tried to avoid the older man for a few days. He saw him in the morning, and Smiley would give him work for the day, but they didn't eat lunch together, even though Smiley asked. Trigger was still ashamed of himself for thinking the worst of Smiley when he was in the shower, and that is how he dealt with it, by avoiding. Smiley was a good friend. A good person, and Trigger hated the fact he'd thought poorly of him, even for just those few moments.

Four nights in a row he slept in the zoo. He was starting to feel more comfortable sleeping there with the animals than in a house. He would have stayed there forever except he promised Sharon he would go back. So he did.

When he left the zoo that day, he wandered the streets as long as he could, as long as the sticky heat would allow. Crews were taking a few of the brick walls down between the burned-out houses on Osage Avenue, stirring up dust and the ashes of the dead yet again. The bricks fell into the light ash, and clouds drifted through the street and into his lungs; he was sucking in the ghosts of MOVE, their ideals and beliefs. It was one of the ways, he supposed, that MOVE survived, by physically becoming part of everyone around them, carried in the lungs, the cells themselves, of every person who walked by 6221 Osage Avenue.

By the time Trigger made it back to the house, the sun was getting low and the city had cooled off somewhat. The maroon van was out front, as well as one of the meth heads, who sat on the front stoop. There was another on the couch, the same spot where Trigger had sat a few days earlier. No lock on the basement door. Up the stairs he saw Sharon in her bed, back facing him, her empty chair in wait. After rinsing his face, he creaked down the hall to his own room. On his mattress on the floor were two of the street dead, a black man and black woman. Both with short, spiky hair. The man was sitting crouched on the edge of the mattress while the woman huddled in a fetal position, staring at nothing with wide, jittery eyes. Trigger was invisible to them. The man talked to no one, aggravated and shaking his hands as he vented and cursed to himself. He would get distracted by his own ideas and start another conversation that lasted until he distracted himself again, causing more frustration.

Trigger was so tired. Always tired. He just wanted that filthy mattress to himself, but there was no way he was going to be able to negotiate them off it. There is no reasoning with the dead. There was room in Sharon's bed, but with Bob home he wanted to avoid another showdown, so he went back downstairs and curled up on the open end of the couch, lightly sleeping while sitting up.

The next morning the corpse on the couch next to him was gone, and so was the one on the stoop. He went upstairs and saw Bob wrapped around Sharon's frail and broken body. The black couple was still in his room, sleeping on his mattress, so he went back downstairs again.

The deadbolt on the basement door was latched and the padlock hung on it, but it wasn't locked. He lifted it in his hand, dense and cool, then slid it off and unlatched the bolt before opening the door. The lights were still on, though it was as bright as midday outside. He broke the threshold and stepped in. The ammonia smell nearly overwhelmed him, and he thought he might actually pass out and crack his head right on those steps.

At the bottom of the steps a shotgun stood propped in the corner, a single barrel, the pump kind. The tip of the long black barrel left scrape marks against the block wall. There were trash bags stuffed full and piled up in several spots, with more trash gathered around them, mostly boxes of cold medicine. On a fold-out table about eight feet long were two small open-flame gas burners, the kind used at a camp site, each off but hooked into a separate bottle of propane beneath the table. Across from that was a wood counter with a sink, the counter stacked with cold pill boxes and pots of liquid. There were other bottles of propane around the room, along with a lot of paint thinner and drain cleaner. Bottles and tubes, gas masks and beer cans, all beneath the glare of the sterile white lights and the hum of a huge fan sucking all the air from the room and out to the rear yard. Only one bag of crystals sat on the table, maybe an ounce, with a pipe next to it. On the other side of the table was a rocking chair with a pillow on the seat, and a small TV atop a wooden box. The room was filthy, and he was disgusted by everything in it and what it stood for.

Trigger picked up the shotgun and eyed down the barrel toward the TV. It was heavy and felt good when he held it. Felt powerful. He put his finger on the trigger, squeezing it lightly just to see what it felt like but not enough to fire it. There was a little black button on the side of the stock, and he slid it back and forth, from white to red, over and over again, to the point he forgot where it was when he started. He eyed down the barrel again at the TV, serious and lasered in on the sight bead at the end. He imagined the TV was Bob, standing there at his mercy, and he felt as tough as he ever did, smiling and saying out loud, "Say hello to my little friend!"—something he always wished he'd had the chance to say. He pictured Bob trembling and begging and himself deciding what would happen. He pretended to pull the trigger, making the gun kick back, and blowing Bob's balls off. He dropped the barrel to the floor, smiled again, then put it back in the corner and went upstairs.

He closed the door behind him and slid the deadbolt, then heard the creak of the hardwood as he walked toward the couch. Halfway down the steps, Bob hung over the handrail, glaring with his ape eyes. Frazzled hair and that key hanging off his chest.

"What the hell?" he said calmly. "What the fuck do you think you're doing?"

Trigger was still so tired. "I wasn't doing nothing."

"Nobody goes down there. Nobody!" he shouted loud enough that if anyone were outside they'd have heard him. The first animal of the day, waking up the jungle.

He was ranting, pumping his fists and screaming, the words pouring down the steps and crashing into Trigger. Only a few of the words hooked together to make sentences anyone might understand, and Trigger didn't really even care if Bob was making sense or not. He was exhausted from the constant clashes and yelling. And just exhausted in general.

While this was going on, Sharon rolled into the hallway. Bob turned his anger toward her and ran up the stairs while yelling at her to get back into the room, and this enraged Trigger, and suddenly he didn't feel so tired. He stepped to the bottom of the stairs and pointed back at Bob, shouting just as loudly, and there they stood, back and forth at each other on a Sunday morning, at the top of their lungs screaming like two monkeys in the trees. The black couple in the bedroom slunk down the hall past Bob—apparently the yelling had roused even them. The man actually said "scuze me" as he tiptoed past. The woman followed, and they swiftly went down the steps and out the door, away from the madness.

Things in the house were so far gone, they'd driven two homeless meth heads out of a free bed.

Sharon reached up and grabbed Bob's arm, anything to try and calm him, but he swung at her with the back of his hand, smacking her right in the nose, seemingly out of reflex, not intentionally trying to hit her.

"Don't you touch her!" Trigger shouted. "Don't you ever touch her again! I know what you do, everybody knows what you do! You touch her again and I'm getting the cops over here!"

That stopped the screaming. Sharon was pinching her nose, and Bob was panting, his chest heaving with short frantic breaths.

"You watch what you say, boy," Bob snarled. "You better be careful what you say."

"I mean it! It's enough!"

The reality is that Trigger wouldn't call the cops, he couldn't. It just wasn't a thing done at that time, not in their neighborhood anyway. Any trust in the authorities evaporated after the bombing, and the thought of Sharon going into foster care handcuffed him, and maybe Bob knew that.

Bob looked at Trigger, then back to Sharon. "You think you're gonna take her away from here? Away from me?" Where you gonna go? You gonna send her to the state hospital? Or maybe you just wanna fuck her!"

He stepped to the back of her wheelchair and grabbed the handles with a rough jerk as if to push the chair forward, down the steps. But even though he was enraged, he paused for just a blink of time, a moment where he struggled to hold himself back, perhaps trying to remember what he used to be. But he couldn't. Lost in his addiction and paranoia, he couldn't find that person, the person who would have reasoned out what he was about to do and stopped it. That person was gone.

"Well, here!" he shouted. "Take her!" He shoved the wheelchair to the edge of the steps and furiously pushed her forward.

Sharon and that chair flew as one for a foot or so, then she lifted from it, arms out, her white gown flowing around her pale skin. For just a flash, she looked almost graceful. Peaceful. Free from the chains of Earth. From her chair, from her captivity. And for the smallest microsecond, she may have even smiled at the feeling. As gravity pulled at her, the smile twisted into an ugly, terrified grimace, like an ethereal ghost barreling down the stairs, screaming to frighten the living, terrified of its own existence. She was helpless. Her arms flailed, as if swimming in the air, while her dead legs lagged. The wheelchair bounced just beneath her, crashing down the bare wooden steps. Above her, Bob saw her hair blow back and the beauty of it, and her billowing gown. Below her, Trigger saw her frightened and hideous expression, and the chrome of the wheelchair as it glinted with each jounce against the steps. He jumped to try and catch her, but everything seemed to be moving in slow motion, like he was pulling against a strong undertow. He made it about a third of the way up the stairs when she fell into him, clawing onto his neck and head, trying to break her fall while the wheelchair simultaneously hit him in the side. They all fell together in an awkward, beautiful dance, all three weightless for just a second and moving as one. Then they hit the steps. Tangled and bouncing from the wood to the plaster wall. Sharon's screams were as loud and chilling as when the truck's grill hit their car. She was so close to Trigger's ear that he couldn't think about the steps against his back, or the steel of the chair digging into him. It was only that voice in his head that he needed to stop.

They rolled over the chair together, her fragile, damaged spine twisting and her dead legs flailing, landing in a tangled pile at the foot of the steps. Bob pointed at them from up above, his chest heaving. He stood, finger out, and something somewhere inside of him thought that maybe he had gone too far, but he couldn't go back, and that hardened voice in his head wouldn't allow it anyway.

"Go ahead! Out . . . get out and stay out!"

Trigger was on the bottom with Sharon between him and her chair. He had to slide out from under both before he could set the chair up and get her into it. His right wrist was in pain, but he just wanted to get her out of the house as quickly as he could.

"Good!" Bob yelled down the steps. "Go live in the zoo with the other animals!"

They made their way onto the front porch, where Trigger looked her over and asked if she was all right. She said she had hit her jaw, that was all, and rubbed at it. She sounded angry.

"You can't do that!" she smacked the palm of her hand on the chair yelling at him, not nearly as loud as Bob, but loud enough so that he knew she was serious. "You can't fight with him like this! All it does is make him mad, and it makes it worse for me, don't you understand that?"

"I'm just trying to help." He had a hangdog look on his face but didn't feel he deserved to be yelled at for trying to do the right thing. He rolled his wrist and stretched his fingers, then flicked his hand to loosen it up. "He can't be doing that. None of this is right. You have to get out of this nuthouse."

She reached into her mouth and wiggled her fingers around some, then pulled out a rotten brown tooth, soft and pitted. She held it up to her eye and looked into it, then flicked it to the sidewalk, almost unconcerned. Trigger watched it arc through the air and bounce off the concrete, then settle in the silt and garbage washed up between the curb and street. He was disgusted. Disgusted with her and Bob and himself.

She went on, unfazed, like she had just brushed a burr from her shirt and now it was forgotten. "There's no place to go. I just have to wait it out. Another year or so and this will all be over."

Trigger shook his head, unsure of what she meant. In a year she would be eighteen and could leave if she wanted without the risk of going into the system. But he also knew that a year was a long time to live like she was living now, a long time to survive. And he thought, maybe, that's what she was saying to him.

He told her about Smiley's offer to stay with him and how he was sure Smiley could help them out.

"I don't even know him, and he don't know me. And do you really want to get him involved with this?" she asked. "Even if he did want to help out, Bob would never allow it. And if I went without him knowing, he'd find out. You know the kind of people he's been dealing with, and if they found out I was with Smiley . . ." The thought of getting Smiley in any kind of danger was enough to let the conversation die.

They sat on the porch for a long while. Trigger noticed the old lady with the cat eyeglasses across the street, again out front, out on her porch. She was looking at them but didn't wave or call hello.

It seemed quiet now inside the house, but he heard other houses, other fights behind other brick walls, and saw other people sitting on their porches. The charcoal smell from Osage Avenue still lingered, a constant reminder of where they lived.

When Sharon felt enough time had passed, she asked Trigger to take her back inside. The basement door was unlocked. She told him to go, and not only to go, but not to come back. She knocked on the basement door and Trigger left. It was the last time he slept in that house.

# Thirteen

THE GLASS SHOWERED OVER HIM, AND HE SAW the weightless dance of the dead. That grill plowing into the side of the car like a sledgehammer, causing permanent damage, the heat of the fire forcing him awake into the heat of another day.

❧

Rabbit rabbit.

❧

It was going to work one day.

❧

It had been a few weeks since the last falling out with Bob. Trigger started buying enough food each morning to last him all day, keeping it in his backpack along with his clothes. He even bought soap and shampoo, but he kept that hidden at the zoo, where he now showered under a rigged-up hose at the back of the maintenance shed, quick and cold, but clean enough and not too bad on hot nights. Naked in the zoo, with the other naked animals.

Even though he hadn't spent the night at the house again, he had stopped in several times to see Sharon and bring her food and some new books and to get a change of clothes. He still did laundry at the laundromat about once a week, but he constantly wore the same clothes and needed to change them.

He could easily just open the front door to check out whether it was safe to go in, and if the basement was unlocked it was usually okay, and if the van was gone it was definitely all right. The more time he spent away, the worse Sharon looked when he went back, the darker and more pungent that morgue of a house was, and the more vacant the dead seemed.

He had run into Bob twice, but Bob hadn't even acknowledged him, and Trigger wondered if Bob even remembered that they'd fought or if Bob even knew who he was anymore. Bob was getting so distant that his line on reality seemed to blur; he just stumbled through each day. He was still pumping out the meth, though, and others still made money off his cook. Trigger found out that he was supplying not only to the local street gang but also to a few individual gang members on the side, including Will Thomas and his uncle, the neatly dressed man he'd seen around a few times, both out front and in the house.

Even though Bob was supplying, he was also using, and because of that, he really wasn't making much money for himself. The more he sold in bulk, the easier it was for him but the less cash he took in. By the time it hit the street, it could have been going for fifty times more than he'd sold it for, but that was a lot of work and Bob didn't want to work that hard. So instead, he lived on the edge of the dead, orbiting around their lives and keeping Sharon there with him like a corpse bride.

Trigger had slept all over the zoo, essentially becoming a full-time inhabitant along with the rest of the imprisoned animals. They were in it together, he and his family, suffering and captive to the will of others. He began to convince himself the animals themselves were concerned for him and his imprisonment, rather than the other way around, like an army of allies watching over him from the shadows.

He began to push the boundaries of what he figured he could get away with, and as each night passed, the zoo felt more and more like his home. He started to see patterns in the security guards' movements, and he would stalk them, using the techniques he saw the animals use. Creeping in camouflage, moving silently, eyes alert and ears tuned in to any foreign sounds. If he was stalking them, they couldn't be stalking him. The only problem was, he had to get a solid, full night's sleep at some point. He was getting fried from the lack of it, jittery, like his nerves and muscles were made of rubber bands pulled tight, tense and constantly quivering.

At least on the days when he worked, he had something to do, and that kept his mind occupied. On days he didn't work, he had to leave the zoo early and just start walking. He walked for hours, alone in his head, fighting real and imagined battles, wearing his joints down just like the soles of his shoes. He didn't realize it, but that much time alone could poison even the strongest person, let alone a lost fourteen-year-old.

Most days he would spend either at the library or in front of the MOVE house. The walls were down now and most of the debris and ash plowed away. The actual MOVE house at 6221 Osage was the first one totally cleaned up. The system wanted it gone as fast as possible, snuffing out their bubbling ideals and opposition before anyone else picked up the torch—and perhaps eliminating any evidence that might tell the real story of what happened that day. There was only a vacant lot left, just a vacant lot with a few echoes whispering the reasons this had happened and how it would happen again if there wasn't change. But only he heard them.

Even though he liked staying at the zoo, the lack of sleep was catching up to him. He considered asking Smiley if he could stay with him for a night or two. He wanted to believe that Smiley would take care of him, but there was still a glowing ember inside that told him not to commit, not to leave himself open for disappointment, and since Smiley hadn't brought it up again, neither did Trigger. Besides, Smiley had been gone from work for three or four days now and never even told Trigger that he was going. At first he thought maybe Smiley had gotten sick, but the temporary manager said he had gone to see his son in San Diego. Trigger was hurt that he had to find out from someone else, as if they were not close enough for Smiley to tell him himself. He had thought they were.

A few days after Smiley returned, they had lunch at the picnic table, and Trigger was happy he was back and that they were spending time together. It was hotter than usual, it felt like the hottest day of an already broiling hot summer, and he hadn't been able to sleep outside the night before. He'd been driven into the reptile house by the heat. There was a service corridor behind the small amphibian tanks where they could feed and remove the animals, and he had lain there on the cool concrete floor, backpack pillow, and slept bone to stone.

After they finished lunch, Trigger sat in the shade of a tree, and Smiley cleared their trash off the table and threw it away, then lay on that picnic table and stared into the clear sky with the sun burning down on him, his skin soaking it up like a worn black sponge. He lay there with his eyes closed and that wide smile across his face.

Trigger watched him smiling, and even laughing to himself a little. He wanted to smile like that, and it made him jealous and angry at how unfair things were.

"Gotta love the sunshine, my son," Smiley said, not opening his eyes. "Why don't you get out that shadow and get some?"

Trigger leaned back against the tree and rubbed his hand across the grass, not answering.

"Come on now," Smiley went on. "Watchu 'fraid of? It ain't gonna turn you black. Least not as black as me!"

Smiley chuckled and roped his fingers together behind his head. Trigger looked at him lying there, enjoying the simplicity of nothing. Finding the joy in just being, in the plainness of a typical day, and he wanted to know how Smiley did it.

They sat in the same place, under the same sun, one of them in it and one of them not. Trigger leaned forward, then dragged himself across the grass into a sunny spot. He lay back and shut his eyes, just like Smiley, the heat on his face and the smell of the steamy earth below him. He could feel the sun through his eyelids and see its powerful light even though his eyes were closed. There were sounds he hadn't heard just seconds before: the birds in the sanctuary, the chatter of people walking past, the electric whine of a maintenance golf cart somewhere farther off. There was a fly so close he could feel the vibration of its wings, and kids laughing as they got ice cream, and beneath all of that was the constant underlying hum of the city just outside the fence.

He laced his fingers behind his head like Smiley did, and it was even more comfortable, and for that second, without even realizing it, he was lying there just like the older man, smiling just like he was. He remained there for what could have been thirty seconds or thirty minutes, he wasn't sure, and it didn't matter that he hadn't slept more than twelve hours in the last three days, he felt good for the first time, maybe for the first time, the only time, in his life that he could remember.

"They have sunshine like this in San Diego?" Trigger asked, grinning because he knew Smiley would love the question.

"Hell yeah, they got this sunshine. Got it every day of the year out there, my son."

Trigger cracked one eye to peek at him but couldn't see his face from where he was.

"I'ma be in that sunshine myself pretty soon, too."

Trigger kept grinning, lost in the rays and getting some needed color to his skin, until Smiley's words ran through his head again.

"You what?" Trigger leaned up on one elbow.

Smiley pulled himself up into a seated position and spun his spindly legs around so his feet were on the seating bench of the table.

"I'ma be in that sunshine pretty soon," he said again. "Full time."

Trigger squinted up at him, and the smile sunk back into its hiding spot, far back in the rear of his mouth, trying to slide down his throat, back into his stomach where it had stayed hidden for so many years, buried with so many other betrayals.

"Full time? What do you mean?"

Smiley pulled his hat off and scratched at the tight curly hairs on his head with his thick fingernails, then slid it back on.

"I wasn't plannin' on telling you, or none of the other guys just yet neither, but since we was talking about it, yeah. I'ma be moving to San Diego. I been out there a few times and was just out there last week for a final interview. I got me a job at the zoo out there. Second best zoo in the country."

His wide smile beamed down, but Trigger could hardly see him. The sun was at its strongest point in the day, set alone in the middle of a deep painted blue sky, but Trigger felt as though a heavy fog had just rolled in, blotting it out and smothering him like it was ash from that fire on Osage Avenue. His lunch gurgled around in his stomach, and he thought for sure he was going to spill it right there, in that steamy earth he was just smiling on a few seconds ago. Smiley looked at Trigger's face and pulled his grin back, rubbing his long waxy fingers together, then he took that deep breath again and blew it out of his nose. "Listen son, I know what you're thinking, but truth is, I gotta do this. My boy is out there, and it's for sure he ain't coming back this way. I gotta try to do what's right for him, what's right for me. He's moving on, forgetting about his old man. I don't mean a lick to him. I gotta do it for him, and for me. I gotta try to make things right, understand?" He stretched his neck from side to side and exhaled heavily through his nose again. "I can't just keep pretending I'm a good father. I gotta go try and be one. For real."

Trigger pushed himself up off the grass and slid back into the shade of the tree. He had to swallow hard, and he felt his lips pucker up and his eyes start to water. A punch right in the stomach.

"Everything's gonna be fine, son. They got a new guy comin' in from Elmwood Zoo—he knows his stuff real good. White boy, just like you." He smiled again, but again it slipped away as fast as it had appeared. Smiley hopped off the table and squatted down beside Trigger. He plucked a long sprig of grass from the ground and tucked it between his teeth and cheek, leaving a few inches hanging from his mouth. He laid that rubber hand on Trigger's shoulder and squeezed.

"I know it's tough, son. Some people got it tougher than others. Rule number one of life—shit ain't fair. Rule number two—go back to rule number one. None of this shit's gonna mean anything if you just keep yo head screwed on straight. You young, white, and smart. You can have whatever you want, believe me, I been there." He hesitated just there, as if he was about to tell Trigger something else.

But then he didn't. "It's like I been telling you . . . you still plenty young. Hell, you just a damn kid still. Just find that smile and you hold onto it."

Trigger pinched the bridge of his nose and squeezed his eyes tight, trying to force back any tears that were welling up.

"You're leaving? You're leaving Philadelphia? Leaving . . ." He wanted to ask if Smiley was leaving *him*, just so he would have to say yes; just to make him uncomfortable so maybe he would change his mind, but he couldn't.

He pulled his hand away from his face and finished the sentence. "You're leaving . . . the zoo?"

They locked eyes, and the sadness reflected back from both sets. Equally shared disappointment, but for different reasons. Smiley dug a finger into the corner of his eye, and for just a moment, it made Trigger feel a bit better, like Smiley was holding back a tear himself.

Smiley stood up and stretched his back, tilting his head toward the sun and crinkling his nose at it. He shook his head like he was shaking off a bad memory, then took a deep breath in and let it out his nose.

"Sometimes," he said, still looking at the sky, "you gotta make tough decisions. It ain't easy. Life is full of hard choices. There are guidelines to follow. This is a tough one for me." He dropped his head but still wasn't looking at Trigger. "Guess it's gonna be tough for you too."

He turned to face Trigger.

"But you ever make it out there to California, you can always come and stay with your Uncle Sam." He reached out his arm and stretched his wide hand to help Trigger up, black as ink on one side and pink on the other. Trigger didn't want to take it and sat there with his arms folded. He didn't care about what Smiley was saying, or what advice he was giving. Smiley was leaving, and that's all he could comprehend just then.

Smiley rolled his fingers and managed to push out a smile, a smile that reached to his back teeth, blade of grass poking out. Trigger finally accepted the hand, and Smiley pulled him to his feet without leaning back, just the strength in his arm. He put his arm over Trigger's shoulder, and they walked back to his office.

Smiley put Trigger on sweeping duty for the rest of the day, and Trigger wandered the zoo, the air humid and heavy. He weaved in and out between carefree, happy people and serious, enslaved animals. Feeling hollow and drained, his insides were as empty and dark as the MOVE house. He wanted to open the cage of every animal he passed, to let every animal in that zoo run wherever it wanted, to let them go free like MOVE had insisted. Even to San Diego. But he couldn't.

He stopped at the giant otters and watched them slide and swim, looking like they didn't have any concerns or troubles. Once when he went with Smiley to clean out the otters' exhibit, Smiley made him wait until the animals were taken out. He said even though they looked like carefree animals having fun, they were aggressive around people and especially territorial. In fact, he said, they disliked people so much that no zoo anywhere had been able to raise giant otter cubs in their exhibits. They could do it if they took the mother and cubs out of the exhibit and kept them away from people, but if they were out there where people were looking at them, pointing and yelling and throwing things, it wouldn't happen. And when zoos had tried to raise cubs in public, that never worked either. The mother otter would ignore the cub, or abuse it, or in some cases even kill it rather than have it be raised in the chaos and noise of the zoo. Was that love or neglect, selfishness or selflessness? Trigger didn't know, but there they were, swimming, sliding, and rolling, keeping all of their issues to themselves. Seemingly carefree, able to continue on despite their internal struggles. He was even jealous of the otters.

He avoided Smiley for the rest of the day, pissed at him and blaming him for the future Trigger saw in front of him, even to the point where Trigger left by the front gate, not the gate at Zoological Drive, the one by Smiley's office, the way he usually did. The crowds were filing out, and the animals stayed locked in. And there he was. The man with the dreadlocks and red megaphone.

He was standing on that same little wooden crate, shirtless and righteous, just like the last time Trigger saw him, tight dreadlocks poking out from beneath the rainbow cap. He was shouting into the megaphone, and it crackled with his rage.

"Long live John Africa! You support this slavery, then you the ones that killed him! Fuck this system! Long live MOVE. Long live John Africa! It ain't right. Let these animals free!"

As before, nervous parents pushed their children past, trying to ignore his rant, and he turned that bullhorn right into their ears, screaming his frustration and blaming them for his anger. He was on fire with drive, relentless to the point where people began to look scared and did their best to completely avoid him, impossible though because of where he perched.

It didn't take long until two security guards from the zoo came out to deal with him. One was a sturdy young black man and the other the older, light-skinned guard who had caught Trigger in the zoo that night. They tried to talk the Rasta off the crate as he continued screaming at the young families leaving. Some children pointed at him, asking their parents questions that they ignored, others just pretended he was a ghost, like he wasn't there and the noise they heard just some random static from the universe.

"How can you own an animal?" he shouted. "Can you own a person? Would that be okay, to lock a bunch of people up in here?

How is one life more important than another? Every life has purpose! How does a man own a river? The moon? No one owns the moon. It's always been. The moon is all of ours! It's mine. It's yours. We all share the universe, we all share the planet. No man gets to own another life!"

When the younger guard couldn't talk him down, the older one stepped up, so close that the bullhorn was no more than two feet from his face, and the Rasta continued yelling into it. Without checking over his shoulder to see if anyone was looking (or perhaps even caring if anyone saw), the guard violently shoved that bullhorn straight back into the Rasta's mouth. It smashed right into his teeth, knocking him backward off the crate and onto the concrete. Mothers tugged at their children's arms, spinning them away. Someone said "Jesus! That's not right!" loud enough for Trigger to hear.

The screaming stopped, and the Rasta lay there, bleeding from his mouth, with that older guard in his sweat-stained zoo uniform looming over him, fists clenched and ready to pounce, almost wanting the Rasta to fight back, just to see if he still had the strength of the enforcer he was when Rizzo had run things.

The man stood up but refused to wipe the blood from his lips. It dripped onto his bare, sticky chest, skin tight to the muscle beneath. Both guards crowded in on him until he finally picked up his crate and started backing away toward the street. People who had just left the zoo's gates and hadn't seen what had happened, saw only a man crowded by two guards and bleeding from the mouth.

"You see?" he shouted over their heads. "You see what you get when you fight this rotten system? You see what you get when you speak up for freedom? Never give up the fight! Long live John Africa! Long live MOVE!"

The man had something to say, and he was going to force people to listen. He was going to force them to change, or get a shot in the mouth trying, but at the very least he would try. But it seemed no one really heard him, his words and thoughts dissipating into the air. Or they didn't *want* to hear him. But Trigger heard those words. Like the Rasta was speaking directly to him. Trigger felt like he was the Rasta's intended target. He worked in that zoo and supported it.

Trigger meandered away with the rest of the crowd, blending in with the tide flowing back into West Philadelphia, but the voice echoed in his head, bouncing from side to side like the elephants marching from wall to wall. That scratchy bullhorn and those red eyes. He was speaking up for those without a voice. He stood alone in a river of listless, callous souls swirling around him, drowning him with indifference. Their instinct telling them to stay clear. And for speaking his mind, for having the courage to defend his values and stand alone in doing it, he got hit in the mouth. And Trigger watched it happen and felt a spark in his belly, felt that maybe he should have been the one taking the punch for his zoo family, they who spent their dark nights watching over him, accepting him and giving him a home.

With the Rasta's words still on his mind, Trigger drifted back to Osage Avenue, sweaty and having more questions than he had started the day with. Although some of the homes were now totally cleaned up, there were still dozens that weren't, dozens that still had the skeleton of the separating walls stretching out of the ash. A few on the outer edge of the fire were only partially damaged but were condemned and would soon come down as well. He saw Will Thomas in the shadow of one of the walls, behind the yellow tape, talking with one of the street dead. He slipped him a tight baggie, and the young man handed over a fist full of bills.

When the man left, Will pulled out a folded-up wad of cash and wrapped the bills around it, then walked back to the street where two other boys his age waited for him, kicking a squashed beer can back and forth. Trigger stared at him, and when Will saw him, he headed right across the street toward Trigger, the other two boys following behind.

"Hey, Nee-Gro! Watchu doing here boy?"

Trigger dropped his backpack to the sidewalk and waited. He'd had enough.

At that, Will barreled forward. He felt Trigger had disrespected him the last time they met, and he had to regain his status. He got right up against him, knocking his shoulder into Trigger's and tilting his head down.

"Who you think you are, yelling at me? Go ahead, you go ahead and raise your voice to me now!"

Will knocked his shoulder into Trigger's again, this time harder, throwing Trigger off balance a bit.

"You wanna give it a go?" Will jumped back and threw his hands up.

Something just flicked on. An electric jolt of heat lighting. The relentless heat of the summer and the beads of sweat trailing from Trigger's neck down his spine . . . the constant taste of ash in his mouth . . . Bob . . . Sharon . . . that bed and her dead legs and the hair on his chest . . . the key . . . the red eyes behind that bullhorn . . . the dead of the city and the dead in the MOVE house . . . Smiley and San Diego . . . His animal instinct kicked in, and just as Will threw those brittle black hands up, Trigger took a massive swing with his balled-up right fist. He hit Will square on his scarred jaw, so hard it hurt Trigger's bony knuckles. It was one swing, one punch. For all of Will's dancing and jabbing at the air, Trigger was the one who threw it, and it was as sure and solid as lead.

Will stumbled back and Trigger swung again, this time with his left, catching him right in the mouth, knuckles right into Will's lips. He didn't even know he could throw a left punch. Will fell to the concrete while one of the two other boys tried to catch him as he went down, hooking him under his arm pits, holding up his limp body, his legs as dead as Sharon's.

"Damn, dude!" the boy said, trying to get Will to his feet.

Trigger stood there, fists still clenched and eyes as red as the Rasta's, the four of them in silence, until Will started grunting and shaking his head a bit, drool and blood pooling in that open pink mouth and dripping from the corner. The boy holding up Will smiled and nodded his head toward Trigger, as if trying to tell him it was something he had wanted to do himself for a long while.

Trigger picked up his backpack and left, drifting down Osage Avenue with an army of spirits of the unseen dead following him.

❧

For about the next week, he didn't see Will or even go to the house at all, splitting his time between the library, Osage Avenue, and the zoo. Most nights he stayed under the bridge in the bird sanctuary, or followed the security guards, especially Myles, the older, light-skinned black. He had found out his name by getting so close to him one night he could hear him called over his radio.

He had become a spy. A spy, working for the other animals. A secret agent, sent to gather as much information on the guards as he could. A predator, stalking. He saw Myles stealing food from the snack shack and pissing in the trees instead of going into the bathroom. Trigger watched stealthily as Myles whistled and hummed to himself, strolling and talking to the animals. Because Trigger knew his routine, it made it easier for Trigger to move around. He could shower behind the maintenance shed without worry of exposure, enjoying the freedom of being nude in the jungle of the zoo. He could eat what he wanted, where he wanted, whether it be a sandwich or a can of fruit he had in his backpack, or something he took from the snack shack. He spent as much time with the animals as he wanted and began talking out loud to them, giving each a distinct voice while he pretended their responses. He was part of that zoo. He was as much an animal in that zoo as any of the others, more so in some ways. They were forced to be there, while he had chosen to be.

Near the end of that week, Smiley introduced Trigger to Smiley's replacement, who was there to start training. Robert, or just Rob. It was too close to Bob for Trigger. Rob had come from the Elmwood Zoo in Norristown, a suburb outside of Philadelphia. Why someone would want to come from outside the city to West Philadelphia made no sense to Trigger. He was shorter than Smiley, and his clothes were tight around his bloated stomach, not like Smiley's loose shirt. He was as pale as Smiley was dark, with square metal-framed glasses. He wore a tie around his fat neck, which Smiley never did, and it seemed too tight. He shook Trigger's hand, and his was small and soft, damp with sweat. He asked Trigger only about work issues, absolutely nothing about his life or himself. He didn't even try to crack a joke to break the ice. He came across as straightforward, dry, and serious. Trigger didn't like him one bit.

Rob followed Smiley around and did what he did. The three of them had lunch together on their picnic bench; Smiley wanted the transition to go smoothly for Trigger and didn't want to just stop doing their lunches together, so he had Rob sit in on one, but Trigger didn't like it at all. Smiley talked about San Diego, but he was the only one talking. It seemed he was the only one excited about the future.

Most of that lunch was flat and foggy; Trigger sat in a daydream, wondering in that idle way that people sometimes do whether, perhaps, if he were to kill Rob, maybe that would force Smiley to stay in Philadelphia.

Each day that week when he woke up in the zoo and waited at the service gate entrance, Smiley was there before Rob. Rob came in with most of the others, on time, floating in together like loose twigs on the banks of a stream, just going where they were pushed. Smiley was there first because he wanted to be, and he pushed against the laziness of the current to do it. On time is late, Trigger remembered Smiley saying.

Trigger started to drift alone. It made things easy. No decisions. That included drifting away from Sharon, and he thought less and less of her the more time he spent away from the house. He soon realized, though, he needed to go back and check on her, so the next day, when he didn't have work, he went there. The van was outside and the door to the house ajar. The vampire couch sat in wait for its next guest, and the basement door was bolted and locked.

He heard voices upstairs so he went up carefully, on the balls of his feet, in the darkness of the daytime, to the top, to Sharon's pen. She sat on the bed with Bob. He was wearing nothing but faded jeans, and she was in the same white nightgown as the last time Trigger had seen her. Bob's shotgun stood propped up in the corner of the bedroom, and Trigger realized that Bob must sometimes carry it around with him from room to room, paranoid, afraid there might be some sudden danger he'd have to face.

The room smelled like rotten meat. There was still smoke hanging in the thick air, and Trigger stood in the doorway watching them, like they were the children and he the adult. Bob and Sharon talked, both at the same time but about different things, and neither listened to the other, and none of it made any sense. They smoked, drank from water bottles, then smoked more. On the desk where books once sat, trash piled up instead, even on top of the hamster's cage.

When Trigger entered the room, they both looked up but didn't stop talking. They scratched at their necks and arms, and there were fresh scabs they picked at, open and oozing. He walked through the room nearly unnoticed, like they had entirely forgotten him and the past. A stranger in the house, a drifting spirit, and they let him roam free.

He cleared the trash off the hamster cage and saw it there, motionless and reeking. It was sunken in, dried up. There was no water in the feeder; it was as dry as hay. He took the cage and went to his room while they continued talking. He held the hamster in his open palm, and alone, where it was safe, he softly cried. He wrapped it in a rag, but before he did, he held it to his lips and whispered to it again, asking forgiveness, then left.

He sat on the front stoop until it got dark out, then moved up to the porch and sat there, eventually falling asleep, just a small cut of carpet between him and the concrete, hamster beside his head.

In the morning he put it into his backpack and walked to the corner store and got something to eat. He got something for Sharon too. He carefully pulled out bills from the backpack strap, looking over his shoulder as he did. After, he stood on the steps of the store, observing the morning. People starting cars and drinking coffee on their stoops, preparing for work and whatever the day would bring them. Some talking, some happy, some aggravated. An entire world of other people who didn't know him and whom he didn't know.

He took out the hamster and unwrapped it a bit. Taking his time, he rubbed its fur, remembering when he first held it, how fragile it had been, how trusting in his palm. He felt the bones of the hamster's corpse in his fingers, then he wrapped it back up and put it back into the backpack. He thought he saw Will Thomas at one point, but the boy headed a different way.

By the time Trigger made it back to the house, it was late morning, and the heat of summer draped across the concrete city. It was August, the most stifling month of the year, and all the city's cement held in the heat. The lock was off the basement door, and Sharon was alone in her room. Trigger brought her a bagel and a soda, setting them on the desk where the hamster cage used to be. She was still in bed, and he sat in her wheelchair. It was worn and broken-in where his back rested, comfortable. He pushed the wheels, rolling himself into the hallway, then backing back into the room. She awoke, then turned over and propped herself up in bed, cracking the soda with a fizz and taking down almost half of it. Her hair looked as brittle as straw, and her skin was thin, marked and ashen, like she had been living underground.

"You took it away?" She flicked her chin up to the empty space on the desk.

Trigger nodded. "I'll bury it, at the zoo."

"I guess I forgot."

She took a small bite of the bagel and chewed softly, then she broke down, her eyes red and clouded. Tears streamed to the corners of her chapped lips. She spoke over the bread in her mouth, sniffing and spitting the words out, wiping her nose with the back of her wrist.

"I'm sorry. I hate this. I hate my life."

She snorted, her mouth open, and he could see the white dough against her gray teeth. She cried uncontrollably as he sat in that wheelchair. She only took one bite of the bagel, and it was a good minute of crying before she swallowed it.

"Let's get out of here," Trigger said, rising from the chair.

She took a big sniff and wiped her face with the bed sheet, sucking any more tears back in, shaking her head. "You know I can't do that. I can't go anywhere. Bob gets my disability, he'll never let that go. I can't just go be homeless, I can't work, I can't even get down the goddamn steps. I'm trapped in here. I'll be trapped in here forever, or at least until I die. Or he does."

"Let's just get out of here for today, I mean. Let's just get outside."

Trigger rolled the wheelchair into the hall and told her to get dressed, then he dragged it down the steps and out onto the porch. By the time he was back upstairs, she had on shorts but no shirt. She sat there half naked and looked paler than he had ever seen her. There were scabs on her chest and bruises on her ribcage and above her hips. She didn't turn away from him; her breasts were small but firm and round like tangerines, and he couldn't look away. He could see her collarbone and how knobby her shoulders were. All of her was just thin white rubber over bone. She had a shirt in her hand but didn't put it on until he turned away, maybe like she wanted him to see her frail and vulnerable. Then he lifted her onto his back, hooking his arms under her dead legs.

Outside, the sun pressed down, and he gently placed her into her chair. She sniffed and rubbed her nose, looking up and crinkling her nose at the sun, just as Smiley had done. A smile started to peel across her face as the sun warmed her.

"Helloooo!" A voice called from across the street.

It was the old woman with the cat eyeglasses, watering plants on her porch.

Sharon squinted across the street, then looked around to see who the woman was talking to. She stuck a finger in her chest, as if asking the woman if she was talking to her. The woman nodded back yes, and Sharon's spirit lifted with the simple greeting. Just from acknowledgment. "Hello!" Sharon excitedly yelled back. She waved her arm as high as she could stretch it, flagging it back and forth to be sure the woman saw. Trigger lifted his hand to near his hip and gave back a smaller wave.

He pushed his sister down the sidewalk, over pebbles and sprigs of weeds clawing up through the cracked sidewalk. They went to Osage Avenue and saw the last bones of the buildings, and to the library where he took her inside for a drink of water. They spent time in the machine-cool air, and she leafed through books about animals and the cities of Europe.

When they left, they went further away from the house. They were in a better neighborhood now, with nicer cars and small fenced-in yards with grass cut tight. There were flowers in pots on some porches. The street felt wider, although it wasn't. On one street, the kids had popped the fire hydrant plug and were running through the powerful spray of city water, cooling down with the wet, white T-shirts sticking to their black skin. Trigger pushed Sharon through the spray, and they both got wet, and they both laughed. Then they stopped and waited in line for water ice, feeling like normal people, and the lemon was so bright and cold it was like running through that hydrant all over again. They nibbled on the tiny bits of lemon peel, and Sharon rubbed the paper cup against the skin of her neck, and they both ate it without spoons. None of it was much, but it felt like everything.

They went back the same way they had left, and he regretted going that way, regretted not going in a different direction, seeing different things. He already knew what waited for him on the same, familiar path.

As they turned onto their street, Will Thomas came up toward them. They both stopped as they met, with Sharon between. Will's hat was pulled low, and he wore heavy, baggy jeans on a brutally hot day. He didn't step up to Trigger, didn't knock into his shoulder.

"You lucky you sister's here, nigger," he said over her to Trigger. "You lucky I got a place to be or I'd drop you right here on the street."

He didn't dance around and jab at the air. He walked past, giving space between them but not looking away as he did. Their eyes locked, and Trigger didn't say anything.

"Next time," he said as he passed, "next time you give me a cheap shot like that, you better hope I don't get up from it. You hear, Nee-Gro?"

Trigger watched him pass, eye to eye, Will's beady glare burning into the center of Trigger's brain. Will kept turning back to glare at him until he was at the end of the block. Trigger never said a word.

When they got close to the house, Trigger checked his watch. They'd been gone for several hours already, but he wanted to keep going, farther and farther. As he pushed her down the street, they both saw Bob sitting on the stoop. He never sat on the stoop. He never went outside and rarely even left the basement, but there he was, no shirt, with that key hiding in his chest hair. He sat scratching his fingers into his dry scalp through that wiry hair, cigarette burning close to his lips. It was unnatural seeing him in the sun, like seeing an opossum in the full light of midday. He wrung his hands and scraped the bare soles of his feet across the rough concrete. When they reached him on the stoop, he pulled out another Salem and lit it with the cherry end of the one he was already smoking, then flicked the butt into the street.

"Where you been?" he asked, staring into the lit end of the cigarette.

Sharon told him that it was such a nice day out that she had asked to take a walk. Bob nodded his head calmly and took a long drag. Standing up, he scratched his hairy belly and stretched his back, locking his fingers behind his neck and smoking hands-free. He stepped down, close to Trigger, who didn't move back. Bob silently took the wheelchair from him and backed it up the steps as gently as he could with Sharon in it, clumping one step over the next until he was on the porch, then backed her inside. She faded from the outside world into the dark abyss of the living room, the dust swirling in the daylight, her pale face the last thing swallowed by the darkness. Bob stepped back outside and closed her in the house behind him, then slowly staggered down the stoop steps. He crowded Trigger, so close that he blew the smoke from his cigarette into Trigger's eyes, but still Trigger didn't back away. Bob nodded and smiled, with the cigarette tipped up. He laid his huge hand, stained with nicotine and dried blood, on Trigger's shoulder. Even though it was bigger than Smiley's, it didn't feel as heavy. All of Bob seemed smaller than the massive frame Trigger remembered. He looked ashen, sallow, and weak. Even still, he towered over Trigger and held more anger than three normal men.

He stepped in as close as he could, stretching out his shoulders to look even bigger. Then that big, scabbed hand slid from Trigger's shoulder, grabbed the back of Trigger's neck, and pulled him in close to his face, cigarette still in his mouth and burning close to Trigger's eye.

"I don't know what you're doing, but she stays here, with me. I warned you before, but you don't seem to get it, so let me make this as clear as I can." He spoke into Trigger's ear, but it wasn't a whisper. "If I catch you with her again . . . if I catch you *here*, again, for any reason, I'll kill you. I'm not talking about just beating the shit out of you. I mean I'll *kill* you. I'll take my gun and blow your balls off. I'll be the one to finish the job."

His thick hand still had Trigger by the back of the neck, holding them face to face, the cigarette dangling there between them, the smoke from Bob's cigarette teasing Trigger's eyes.

Two people walked down the sidewalk coming from different directions. One of them, a middle-aged, stocky black man wearing a tight black tee shirt spoke up when he got close to them. "Yo man . . . yo . . . what'r you doin with that boy? Don't you be handling him like that."

Bob released Trigger and stepped directly into the man's path.

"I'm minding my own damn business. You better do the same. Or do you wanna get involved?" Bob glared at him, locking eyes and stretching out his back to show his full size.

The man said, "That ain't right," but veered into the street to avoid any further confrontation. The man kept looking back at Bob, who kept staring him down, until he was well past and could get back on the sidewalk. As soon as he did, Bob's hand was back on Trigger's neck, pulling him close again.

The feel of that hand against his skin made Trigger wince. It wasn't the hand of a proud father on his son after having a catch. It wasn't a hand pulling him in close, giving sage advice or direction—it was the hand of a dangerous stranger. Uncomfortably close. Callous. Menacing.

Bob leaned back and stepped a foot away. He pulled the cigarette from his mouth, flicked it into the street, and smiled at Trigger, who should have been afraid. He knew Bob was serious, he knew he was unhinged enough to do it, but even still, he wasn't afraid. He was as calm as the pond water in the bird sanctuary. He didn't move back, or swallow, or even look away. He stood right there, fourteen years old, so close he could smell Bob's rotten teeth even with the cigarette smoke swirling around them. He stood solidly, all five-foot-six, one hundred twenty pounds of him, in front of that haggard football player and spoke the truth as he saw it.

"She won't be here much longer. I can guarantee you that."

Bob stepped back to the stoop and ran the chain around his neck through his chapped lips and nodded, "Uh huh . . . and how you gonna guarantee that? You gonna go in and get her?" He turned sideways and held his arm to the door, inviting Trigger to enter. "Go ahead. Go ahead in and get her. See what happens."

Trigger was tempted to take him up on it, but if he went in, he doubted he'd be coming back out. He didn't want to let Bob have the last word, so he just reached for whatever he had in his head.

"No, I'm not gonna go in. But maybe someone else will. Maybe some people who are interested in what's in the basement, you think? Maybe I make a call and some people show up here and find out what's been going on in that basement of yours. What you been doing down there."

Ratting someone out was a serious threat in their neighborhood, and bringing the authorities into their world was, to many, unforgivable. Bob stepped up the stoop onto the porch and turned back to Trigger, running that key up and down that chain.

"If you go that route," he said, "you not only get yourself killed, but you get her killed too. And that, *I* can guarantee." With that, Bob headed back into the house and closed the door behind him.

# Fourteen

THERE WEREN'T A LOT OF THINGS TRIGGER could remember from early in his childhood. His earliest clear memory was the crash. Other things surely happened to him, bad and good, before then, but the crash was the first thing he could recall. The crash endured in his mind, vivid, though he only had bits and pieces of what happened after that. Just shards and flashes of images and faces, words and sounds. Like remembering his mother in the front seat, tangled in with the metal and glass, jammed so deep she was part of the machine. The gas fumes so strong he was sure that alone was enough to kill her.

He was so young he hardly knew her, but the crash and her loss shadowed him his entire life.

People were trying to pull her out through the window, but her legs were crushed so tightly they could only shift her a few inches. The flames started creeping in from under the dash, burning her feet and legs, and he smelled the charred meat.

She threw her head back and screamed, pounding the steering wheel so hard he was terrified of her. Beneath that, he heard Sharon moaning. She wasn't screaming out of control like his mother, just swimming with the pain as best she could. Once those flames grew wild and the smoke billowed to the rear of the car, black and angry, and the people realized they weren't going to be able to get his mom out of the car, they turned their attention to him and Sharon. For those few seconds, the time it took them to get from the front doors to the rear, his mother was alone in that front seat, burning alive. She looked back in screaming agony at him, looked to him with those wild eyes for help, and he saw those flames roll over, insatiable and indifferent.

By the time they got him out, the screaming had stopped.

When they'd gotten Sharon out as well, their mother still remained wedged in tight, and it was too hot for anyone to attempt to reach her. They watched those flames lick out of the windows, and although she was hidden in a blanket of fire and smoke, Trigger and Sharon both knew she was locked in that front seat, charred.

Both he and Sharon were sent off in separate ambulances. There was a young man in Trigger's. He sat face to face with him for the ride, telling him how tough he was. Trigger wanted to ask him why. Why was he tough? All he did was sit in the back seat of a car that got crushed, then wait there until someone took him out.

The only other thing he really remembered was getting a needle in his forehead before they stitched him up. It was so precise, a burning dot, so small but so painful. No memory of how he got home or who drove him or what he did the rest of that night.

Sharon wasn't there at their mother's funeral. He hadn't been allowed to see her for weeks, until someone finally took him to the hospital. It was then he found out she would never walk again. She laid in bed, distant and bitter. He was too young to totally comprehend the magnitude of her situation. It would take years for him to fully accept it. She never did.

Trigger hadn't been allowed to go to the cemetery, but there was a small gathering at the little house in Swathmore they lived in. There were people rubbing his head, looking at his stitches and again telling him that he was tough, which he still didn't understand. People were eating, and he heard some people laughing and slapping other people on the back. Bob was there. It was one of Trigger's first memories of him. Not shirtless or with frazzled hair or clouded eyes. Just a big, strong man, standing like a stone carving. He looked impervious to the damage, but he wasn't. He was just acting strong so others could stay strong. Inside he was crushed and as afraid as a lost child. Not long after, they moved to West Philadelphia, and Trigger never saw any of those people again. Or that Bob.

❧

He was no longer staying at the zoo because he wanted to—now he had to. He had no place else to go. He knew the three night security guards were near the wolf habitat at the far end of the zoo, away from the main gate, so he had no problem strolling behind the maintenance building, pulling out his stashed shampoo, and stripping down. He rigged the hose up to a hook on the block wall of the building and clipped the nozzle on *spray* and showered. It was cold as always, but he was so hot and sticky with sweat he didn't mind. It made him feel fresh, alive, and clean. It cleared his thoughts, and for that short time, all he thought of was that cold water on his hot skin. When he finished, he dried himself off with a small towel he kept in his backpack, and then put on the same clothes (which made him feel a bit less clean).

He planned on sleeping in the bird sanctuary again, under the bridge. He was starting to like sleeping under the bridge, like it was his own little home where no one else ever came. He planned on burying the hamster there. There, in what he now thought of as his pen, Trigger's pen, right beneath that bridge. He dug a small hole in a mulch bed, right next to the bridge, and laid it in. As he began to cover the dry gray fur, he stopped. Half of the hamster was still exposed. It didn't feel right to him. He pulled it out and filled the hole back in, then went back to the wolf habitat. There, he crawled under the fence, and just outside, he dug another hole in the earth with a stick, buried the hamster, then slipped back in.

Not far off the main walking path by the entrance was the polar bear exhibit, and on his way back to the bridge, Trigger heard splashing. The zoo had only one polar bear, Charlie. Charlie had come to the zoo at the age of four, bright white and curious. He was the first polar bear the zoo ever had. They built an enclosure for him that included a grassy area and a concrete pool, with a thick plexiglass front. On the exterior there were steps where people could walk down a gentle grade and walk up to the glass to watch Charlie swim. It was always crowded, and when he jumped into the water, the kids would press their faces against that glass.

Trigger followed the sound, and sure enough it was Charlie in his pool. Typically he didn't move around much at night. He had been at the zoo for almost ten years now, and Smiley said he hadn't been acting right over the past few, but nobody seemed to really know why. Still, as long as he swam, the people would continue coming to see him. His coat wasn't bright white anymore but singed with yellow, and when he walked, he shook his head constantly, wagging it back and forth, a never-ending *no*. He was thin, thinner than you would think a bear should be, and his face seemed like it was drooping, like it was made of clay and losing the eternal battle with gravity. There was a blue plastic barrel in the water, and during the day, they would throw big blocks of ice in the water for him to play with. But now, at night, with no one there, he was just floundering in that lukewarm water, swatting that blue barrel around by himself. When he had first arrived, the keeper would hide food in his exhibit for him to hunt for, but over time, they just started throwing it in there, wherever, and he would just walk over and eat it, then go back to shaking his head and pacing. Pacing, just like the elephants, or Trigger on Osage Avenue.

Charlie was the only one of his kind in the zoo, solitary. It looked to Trigger like he was lonely, and although he was massive and had complete dominance in his world, loneliness could crush even the most powerful and determined spirit.

♣

Rabbit rabbit.

If he didn't say it for one day, that would be the one day it would work, and he'd miss out.

♣

After the grill once again smashed into the side of the car and the flames had licked their way back to him, he woke to the sound of the birds and the riffling water. For about twenty seconds he forgot who he was; it was like when he had smoked the meth.

It felt hotter than usual, if that was even possible, and he had overslept, which was rare and potentially risky. Two voices carried across the water. Walking down the path and stopping on the wooden bridge, right over his head, were two keepers. They were talking about one of the birds that might have feather mites, and if it did, how big of a problem it might be. One infected individual could contaminate an entire aviary. They waited there quietly until they heard a thin squawk, and one of them said, "That one," then their footsteps clumped off the bridge. Trigger slung his backpack on and peeked out. No one to be seen. He scrambled to the path and walked calmly out of the exhibit. There were already workers preparing for the day, but once he was on the walking path, no one knew where he had come from.

Trigger had a meeting scheduled first thing with Rob, the new maintenance manager taking over for Smiley. Maybe somewhere in the back of his mind, he was trying to avoid the meeting. Maybe if he didn't go, somehow Smiley wouldn't leave, and that was why he'd overslept.

In the maintenance office, Smiley sat in the chair in front of the desk, where Trigger usually sat. Rob sat in the desk chair behind it. Smiley's chair. There was an open box of doughnuts with only two left, both plain, the kind people dip into coffee. Rob was meeting with each of the maintenance crew members separately, to get to know them, as he said. "Last one in gets the leftovers," he joked, pointing at the box. Just because of that, Trigger didn't want to take one, but he was so hungry that he did anyway, though he resolved to eat it only after he had left.

Rob gave Trigger his work detail for the day. It was shit patrol in the primate reserve, probably the worst job in the zoo. "The early bird gets the worm," Rob continued, "and the late bird gets the shit." He winked at Smiley, who kept a flat face, then Rob told Trigger to come back to the office for their meeting over lunch since it was too late to have it just then.

While the primates were outside in their jungle-style exhibit, the doors that allowed them back into the indoor exhibit area were shut, so Trigger could clean the interior pens. Each had three concrete walls, a concrete floor, and a barred, open cage front a safe distance away from where visitors could watch the animals while they played with some ropes and a tire hanging from the ceiling, or just lay in the piles of straw on the floor. He had to dig through the straw and shovel up the shit from those apes, then bring in new straw for them to sleep in. The shoveling of the shit wasn't the worst part. The worst part was the heckling of stragglers who hung around the inside while the animals were outside. Their laughter ricocheted off those walls, each laugh punching him in the gut. Sometimes they told him to make sure he didn't miss any shit, and sometimes they would say he was the ugliest gorilla in the place. Usually it was just kids acting out because they had a few minutes away from their parents and wanted to impress each other, but sometimes it was an adult, trying to do the same with other adults. Playing the alpha. Thinking they were better. But in reality they were no different from the apes themselves, just posturing, trying to look big. He stood there and took it, behind the bars of the cage, like every other animal in the zoo.

Every one of them, he pretended to be friends with, to talk with, each one he whispered to about his problems, was ultimately at the mercy of a keeper, and that was how he was beginning to feel. And he thought they must be feeling the same way. Restless, stifled, and rebellious. The Rasta was right. MOVE was right. The difference was, he could walk away. And he did. For the first time, he left a job incomplete, just to get out of that cage. It was the first assignment Rob had given him, and he blew it off.

When Trigger met up with Rob for lunch, Smiley wasn't there. Rob sat behind the desk marking some things down with a pencil. He asked Trigger to sit without looking up, pointing to the chair with the eraser end of his pencil, then returned to writing as Trigger sat in silence. He went on writing just long enough that it started to feel uncomfortable, and the longer it took, the more Trigger resented him sitting in that chair. Smiley's chair. Using Smiley's pencil. He felt Rob was taking everything away. Not only taking everything away from Smiley, but taking Trigger's salvation. Rob was just a man, a man only there doing a job, but Trigger now saw him as the enemy.

Just as Trigger was about done picking at his fingernails, just when he thought he would explode and jump across the desk and stab Rob in the heart with that pencil, the new supervisor put it down and looked up at him.

He had a fatty, almost perfectly round head, with sparse strands of hair raked across the top. He wore wire-rimmed glasses that looked too small for his thick face and pinched him at the nose just tightly enough that he was constantly removing them to massage his bridge. A white shirt stretched uncomfortably across his huge belly, and the red tie he wore looked like it was cutting into his neck.

He pulled his glasses off and dropped them onto the desk, massaging the red indentations with his thumb and forefinger. "So," he said, "Sam tells me you're a real hard worker. Never late and never missed a day. That sound about right?"

Trigger had just missed several days, and he didn't know if Smiley had told Rob that or not, so he decided to not say anything.

Rob continued, tapping the tip of his pencil on a chart that sat on his desk and slipping his glasses back on. "Looks to me like you been putting in a lot of hours. More hours than a kid of fourteen should be working, if you ask me." He looked up at Trigger with powder blue eyes, about as opposite to Smiley's as you could get. "A fair amount of hours, all right."

Trigger still sat quietly, scratching at the back of his hand and wanting only to get out of the room. To get away from Rob.

Rob leaned in closer, his belly pressing into the desk. "Don't you want to be hanging out with your friends in the summer? Playing sports and whatever? Not just sitting here with a bunch of dumb animals all week. Right?"

"I like the animals."

Rob leaned back in his chair, Smiley's chair, and it creaked under his weight. "I'm sure you do. Anyway, I do things a little differently than Sam does. I ran a pretty tight ship at Elmwood. I'm telling you, just like I'm telling the rest of the guys. Things are gonna be different around here from now on. Just because you're the youngest, you won't be treated any differently. I'm also cutting down on unnecessary hours and overtime around here. There are a lot of other guys who need the work more than you do, I would imagine. I'm dropping you to two days a week, six-hour shifts. After we see how that works out, maybe in a bit you get a few more hours. Sam says you're a good worker and all, but some of the guys here have families. They need those hours to live on, not just for gum and comics and movies or whatever. Understand?"

He once again removed his glasses, rubbed the bridge of his nose, then stuffed his glasses back on his face. "Anything you want to ask me? Now's the time."

Two days a week meant Trigger would have to be up and out of the zoo almost every day early, earlier than when the first shift started coming in. He needed that money too, and not for movies and comics. For food. To do his laundry. For Sharon.

Rob's decision was going to make his life a lot tougher. He had gotten to where he had some stability at the zoo, almost to the point of feeling comfortable. He'd gotten to where he felt secure, and now it was getting disrupted. Things were going to be different, Rob had just said, and different could be bad. Trigger was afraid of losing what little he had, the new home he had created for himself, that helped him survive, that gave him guidelines. His new family that looked out for him and that he looked out for.

He wanted to ask Rob to leave. He wanted to ask him to let everything stay the way it was. He wanted to ask him to let Smiley stay. But he asked him nothing.

"No? Good. Okay then, let's get back to it." Rob stood up and stretched out that waterlogged hand, and Trigger pressed his into it. It wasn't large or hard like Smiley's; it was just a fat sweaty little hand. Trigger left, and they never even had lunch.

As soon as his shift ended, Trigger left through the front entrance with the rest of the debris floating out of the zoo, joining the river of people, lost in the hum of their meaningless chatter. The MOVE follower with his rastacap wasn't out there. He wanted the man there, to hear his words, to see his red eyes. He wanted to be part of it, and he thought, for just a second, maybe he could be the one screaming into the crowd about freedom, about right and wrong. Trigger wanted to be above them all in that river, like a boulder they could cling to—he could be the one to make change. But he was just a boy, and that was just a daydream. Still, at least he *wanted* to do it, so he thought maybe someday he could.

He had hours to kill before he could sneak back into the zoo, so he went to the library again to escape the heat. The librarian started to notice him spending more time there, and the books that he checked out for Sharon, the ones Bob had burned, were never returned. When she watched him enter, he felt as if she knew what happened to them, but he reasoned that was impossible. After that, he went back to Osage Avenue.

The spirits had wandered off into other areas of the city, caught in the pull of the unknown, but they likely weren't gone for good. They would be back; they didn't have a choice in the matter.

He sat on the stoop across the street staring into that vacuum, staring into an idea, a seed taking root but pulled before it fully sprouted. He sat there in a haze for close to an hour, his mind under the constant influence of loneliness and turbulent emotion. He sat a long enough time for the sun to burn off its anger and mellow into a soft glow before he started off, back to the zoo.

Once he moved away from the MOVE house, the brick walls returned, sixty-one of them, with the charred remains of other lives. In the rubble of those homes, there were still metal bed frames and pipes reaching out of the debris. There were still blackened rafters and singed stuffed animals and the broken glass of family photos. He really didn't care too much about those lives, though he thought maybe he should. But he didn't live the lives in those homes.

Just as the sun dipped below the city skyline and the sky had turned to smoky dusk, the streetlights on the surviving side of the street kicked on. Trigger heard two quick pops. He was coming up on an intersection where two partially gutted homes stood, still looking mostly like someplace people had once lived. He was the only person on the street, the heat of the day had forced everyone else inside. *Pop. Pop.* He stopped where he was.

Growing up in West Philadelphia, he'd learned the sound of a handgun fairly early on, hearing it at least once every few months from his bedroom. He leaned against a long, faded black car across the street from the yellow caution tape from where he'd heard the shots. No more than twenty seconds later, he saw Troy Thomas turn the corner, walking fast but not running, walking heel to toe, trying to gain as much ground as he could without breaking stride. He wore a blue shirt with the red Superman logo on it. Troy's afro was round as the top of a mushroom, and Trigger could see his nearly yellow face, too old and mean to have the baby fat that it did.

When Troy was far enough away, Trigger crossed the street. There were still fire-damaged cars parked alongside other miscellaneous bits of charred remains. Any parts of the houses that had survived the fire had been looted and picked clean, most within hours, before the ashes had completely cooled. Before the owners could return, the living dead had swarmed in like a hoard of bees and taken anything of value that had not been burned up. Even if it had only sentimental value, some heartless lost souls would rather take something and throw it away later than let someone else have it. They lived only for themselves. There was nothing else in their universe except for those *wants*, and they swirled around death without enough compassion or love to care, straddling the line between life and afterlife, almost existing in both at the same time.

Trigger crept down the street, carefully listening for more pops. There was nothing. Burned out dreams and empty lots.

When he turned to go back and continue to the zoo, he heard what he thought might have been a voice, thin and desperate, coming from inside one of the damaged homes. He believed it was a voice, but with the fading light of the sun casting shadows over the graves of West Philadelphia, it could have easily been a stray cat growling for some food, or nothing at all except his own thoughts teasing him again. He could have walked on and never known what the sound was but chose a different path. He took the path that led him to follow that frail sound.

Picking his way into the corner house, he let his eyes adjust to the darkness like animals do. He hadn't made it into that death trap more than six feet when he heard that sound again, but this time he knew it was a voice, and that made his heart hammer.

"Heyyyy . . ." he thought he heard, and he imagined a ghoul coaxing him closer. He did one quick scan over the black carbon scraps that made up the floor, but it looked flat and dead.

"Hel . . ."

Now he became scared, not sure of what he had just heard. Scared like the first night he'd slept in the zoo. Not afraid of what might really be there, more afraid of what he didn't understand, the unknown.

He looked across the scorched rubble again and, among the poking pipes and scalded memories, saw a hand. It was raised up, like a kid in school waiting to be called on by the teacher. Fingers splayed out against the backlight of the dying sun. It moved. No more than twenty feet away, waving him down. He sucked up all the courage he could, then stepped lightly through the ash of the dead.

"Hellllpp . . ." It wasn't hey, or hell; it was *help*. A breathy voice, calling lightly, calling for help.

There, crumpled in a pile of black wood and twisted copper, lay Will Thomas. He was as gray as the ash around him. His Phillies hat was a few feet away, and there were a few dollar bills carving a trail between it and him. Even as Trigger knelt beside him, Will kept his arm in the air, calling to anyone within earshot, anyone who might find him. With his other hand, he squeezed Trigger's forearm hard, clinging to a lifeline. There were two red splotches on his baggy T-shirt, lower left side. He was breathing fast, clearly panicked, his eyelids stretched wide and eyes rolling around in his head, confused and frightened. A wounded animal looking for a corner to back into.

He clung to Trigger's arm, holding on to the only hope he had.

"Trey. Trey, help me. Please. Help me."

There was no knocking of shoulders, no dancing and throwing jabs at the air and trying to impress. It was just a terrified kid in the dirt of a burned-out house, bleeding to death.

Trigger told him he would go get help, and even as he got up to look for it, Will held onto his arm. Trigger had to pry it off and stumble through the charred clutter to make his way out. He saw the arm still held up stiff, beaconing to anyone who happened by, but no one else did.

Once outside the building's remnants, Trigger ran toward Osage Avenue, then slowed. Then walked. He knew every second was important, and he let them drain away with Will's blood. His pace slowed, and he considered the situation. Will needed him. Trigger controlled his destiny. For all the times he'd been degraded, all the times he'd been beaten and humiliated, now it was his turn. Trigger's turn to decide the outcome. He was the king of the pride. He had waited and hoped to be in this position for years, and now it was here.

Still, he knew how it felt to be at someone else's mercy, and it felt like total shit. Even though Will had tormented him relentlessly, by the time he reached the other side of the street, he came to realize that treating Will the same way he had been treated didn't make him feel any better. In fact, it made him feel worse. It didn't give him strength, it made him feel weak, and he didn't know he could feel any weaker than he already did. And that meant he had to have some strength in him that he had never realized. *Each life is dependent on every other life, and all life has purpose.* John Africa said that. There are guidelines we're supposed to follow. The circumstances that put Will in this place in life were beyond his control, they weren't all his fault.

Trigger decided to do what was right and, in doing so, not only changed the outcome of Will's life but his own as well—he just hadn't yet realized it.

Trigger picked up his pace, breaking out of his pondering walk and into a panicked run, rushing from stoop to stoop, pounding and shouting for help on the doors of the homes that still stood on the living side of the street. But most people in that neighborhood had learned over time not to open doors or get involved in business that was not theirs. He finally found a woman who agreed to call 911, then shut the door behind her, leaving Trigger alone on the street. He anxiously waited for help to arrive, knowing more of Will's blood seeped into the earth with each passing minute, but he couldn't go back and wait with him, Will had to do it alone. Trigger had to wait for help and bring them to Will, to be sure they could find him. Trigger paced the street, constantly looking for approaching headlights.

After what seemed like an hour but couldn't have been, a cop rolled up. Trigger flagged him down, and the cop followed him to Will, his arm still upright like a flagpole. The officer told Trigger to wait by the car, but as soon as he had the chance, Trigger slipped away. He knew enough not to answer any questions about what he'd seen or heard, or even who he was. Once it was in their hands, there was nothing else he could do to help. It would only make things worse if he stayed.

He didn't get far, only about a half a block, when he found a dark corner of an alley where he could stay hidden but still see the lights of the cop car bouncing off the brick buildings. Soon after, he heard the sirens and a fat, wide ambulance rumbled down the street. The activity had some of the neighbors pulling up windows and peeking outdoors, but besides Trigger, there wasn't a soul out. He saw the stretcher loaded into the back of the ambulance but had no idea if it had a scared young boy on it or a corpse, his soul cursed to drift along Osage Avenue in the river of other lost souls.

# Fifteen

HE SAW HER HEAD JOLT HARD TO THE LEFT, cracking into the window and, at the same time, the thick rusted grill of that truck blasting through the glass and knocking it back the other way. Two forces colliding. The smell of gas overpowering, and the sound just as potent. There was screaming and panic, and those flames crept up again. Then the heat got so great it forced him awake, just like every other day.

⁂

Rabbit rabbit.

Every morning.

It would summon the good luck someday.

⁂

It was getting harder to sleep in the zoo. The mornings when he had to work, it was not a problem, but those days had been cut. The rest of the time, it was more difficult. He could still get in at night and move around easily enough, getting in and out of places with the master key, but leaving in the morning without being spotted was becoming tougher. Rob had done what he called a "perimeter check" of the fencing around the zoo and found where Trigger had cut the fence ties to get in. It hadn't yet been fixed, but Trigger knew it was on Rob's list. After that he would be down to just using the service entrance on Zoological Drive or the 34th Street entrance, and that could get hairy. Each morning before he went to the maintenance room to send the guys off for the day, Rob would wander the zoo. He was just checking on the general condition of things, but Trigger's unjustified distrust would have had him bet his meager paycheck that Rob was searching the grounds for him. Hunting him down.

This morning was a Friday, Smiley's last day at the zoo, and Trigger was scheduled to work. At the end of the day, there was going to be a goodbye party. Trigger was so upset he thought about skipping it and never saying goodbye or seeing Smiley again, but he didn't have the heart.

After the zoo closed, everyone gathered in the picnic area where they used to have lunch together. There were dozens of people there, laughing and rubbing Smiley's neck and drinking punch spiked with rum as the sun edged lower. It reminded Trigger of his mother's wake. Who were these people? Did they even know Smiley? Trigger had never even seen most of them, all these people who laughed and congratulated Smiley, happy for the free drinks and food. But Trigger was still upset. Even Rob was getting drunk, and he took a moment to call everyone's attention and make a speech about how much they would miss Uncle Sam, and how when he went on to become rich and famous in California, not to forget about them back here in Philadelphia. He hadn't even known Smiley for two weeks and he acted like they were brothers, and that burned Trigger up.

There was a big cake in the shape of an elephant, Smiley's favorite animal in the zoo. It was white with a blue-frosted border and speckled with candles. When it came time to blow them out, Smiley looked around, twisting his neck over the crowd of people.

"Where you at, son? Get over here an' blow these out. Where Trey at?"

Some people parted, making a corridor from him to that cake. Trigger wanted only to crawl into a hole in the ground like one of the prairie dogs, but people clapped and pushed him toward the wooden picnic table, where he reluctantly bent down and blew out those candles. It felt like he was blowing out his entire life, and it took all his strength not to blubber and spit all over that cake. There was some writing on it in blue frosting as well, and even though it was no more than six inches from his face, he had no idea what it said. Smiley cut into the cake and handed him the first piece, the trunk of the elephant, on a little paper plate.

People ate and drank some more, and then the group thinned out. Not long after the punch was gone, so were most of the people. Myles was still there, and a few others, but Rob had gone. Trigger sat in the shade of that tree, cake untouched in his lap.

"Get out the shadows, son." Smiley called. He reached that wide hand out and pulled Trigger up to his feet. They walked out of view of the few stragglers left, and Smiley turned Trigger around to face him. The older man's eyes squinted with rum, causing deep black crevasses in the corners, smile stretching his lips.

"Listen," he said. "Things are gonna be different around here now. Things gonna change for you. But sometimes, change is good, right?" He held his pink palms to the sky and shrugged his shoulders, then dug in the pocket of his billowy shirt and pulled out a folded paper. "Three things I gotta go over with you. First, on here is the contact for the Covenant House of Pennsylvania. Place right in

North Philly. They can help out, give you a place to go if you need it, you understand?" He dipped his head and looked at Trigger from the corner of his eye. "They good people there, believe me, I know. I spent time there when I was about yo age. Help you get on yo feet if you need it. Next, on here is my new address and number in San Diego. We family. We there for each other. If you ever get out that way, you look up your Uncle Sam. Maybe someday, you could even come work for me again out there, in the San Diego Zoo. Second best zoo in America."

He pressed the paper into Trigger's palm and closed his heavy hands around it.

"Now," he said, "the third thing. I need something from you."

"What do you need from me?"

Smiley stepped back and twisted his head from side to side, scanning the area, making sure they were alone. "I need my key back," he said, holding his palm out flat in front of Trigger. "I didn't say nothin' cause you gotta do what you gotta do, but I only got four of those master keys, and I got to return every one today. If not, they got to re-key this whole place, and I gotta pay for it."

Trigger's first reaction was to deny even knowing what Smiley was talking about. The man couldn't prove he had the key, at least Trigger didn't think he could. But for him to stand there and lie into Smiley's eyes, make a fool out of him, Trigger couldn't do it, and he was proud of himself that he didn't.

The key was still in that yellow plastic change holder in his back pocket. It opened when it was squeezed, and snapped shut when released. The most valuable thing in his life, and he kept it as close as possible. At that moment, he realized he was perhaps too much like Bob. Bob's key was chained around his neck like a noose, while Trigger's was like a brick of lead he dragged around, wanting it for protection at the cost of carrying that weight.

He dug it out and handed it over to Smiley, stuffing the paper into the change purse in its place, and returned it to his back pocket. Smiley pinched the key by the teeth, holding it up between their eyes, shaking it in his leather fingers.

"You a man. You don't need to be living in no zoo."

They talked a few more minutes until someone called Smiley over to say goodbye. While Smiley's back was turned, Trigger slipped away.

He wandered to Osage. The cleanup of the destroyed homes was close to completion. There was nothing new just yet, no newly constructed dreams waiting to be torn down, but the scraping away of the dreams of past lives was almost complete. The rest of the world had moved on, and for most everyone except the people in and around the city of Philadelphia, the MOVE bombing was already disappearing from their memories like a thin wisp of smoke. Other issues arose, grabbing the headlines and people's interest instead, these also as quickly forgotten, until it all happened yet again. The cycle never ending. But it wasn't a memory for Trigger. He was living in it, and he didn't want to forget, even though he felt it draining him. He knew it was meaningless, and he knew he was becoming obsessed with it, and he wasn't even sure why. He knew only that a group of people had recently lived here, lived with ideals and principles and guidelines. And they were gone because others just couldn't abide how they didn't fit in, how they didn't want what people around here were supposed to want.

On the way back to the zoo, he walked past his house, stopping on the stoop across the street and looking into the windows of what used to be his room. Muffled music worked its way into the street, and a few of the living dead drifted in and out. He pictured Sharon, hearing that same music, alone in her bedroom. At least he hoped she was alone.

"Hello," a thin voice spoke. Behind him, in the doorway to her house, was the old woman with the cat eyeglasses. He didn't even realize he was sitting on her stoop.

"Oh," he said. "I'm sorry. I was just sitting here a second and . . ."

He stood to leave.

"It's all right," she said. "You're the boy from across the street. Right?"

He nodded and considered if that was a good enough response. He took a step, as if to leave, wanting their conversation over so he could get back to his own thoughts, but he didn't. He dug up the strength and walked up her steps, right onto her porch and to her door. He stuck out his hand.

"I'm Trey. Sorry I haven't said hi to you before."

She walked onto the porch and closed the door behind her. Her hand was soft when she took his and shook it. Skin thin, like it might tear away if he was too rough with it. Nothing like Smiley's hand.

"I'm Dottie," she said. "It's nice to finally meet you."

The exchange was direct and pleasant and for some reason, when it was done, Trigger felt better than he had before it. She slipped back behind her door, and he crossed the street.

He started up the steps of his house, but when the door opened he backed off. It was just one of the dead carried away by his own harsh fate, but Trigger pictured Bob in there tweaked out and holding his shotgun and figured it would be a better play to wait until the place had quieted down before he went to check on Sharon.

Back at the zoo, he pulled up the chain-link fence and squeezed under it. Without his key, he was forced to stay outdoors all night. He brought in his own food, he could no longer get into the snack shack if he wanted. At least he was safe from the animals outside the zoo fence.

Once he found where Myles was, he knew how to avoid him and could wander somewhat freely, almost like a visitor. He meandered from exhibit to exhibit, feeling more guilt with each trapped animal he looked at and feeling terrible when they looked back at him, eye to eye. He thought it was strange, how every animal was a different shape and size and makeup, but nearly all had two eyes, just like him. About the same size, color generally the same, and seeing things pretty much the same way he did. He could see it in those eyes that they were jealous of him. They wanted his freedom; but what they saw as liberty he knew was just a different kind of cage. He wanted to set every one of them free, but if he did, they would be out of his life forever.

He went to the bird sanctuary, curled up under the bridge, and listened to the water and the caged birds around him. The sounds were washing away all the memories of Sharon, and of Smiley. He began to slip away into his other world, but he didn't want just to be lulled asleep, he didn't want to hide under the bridge, invisible. He crawled out and walked right down the path, careless, not looking out for Myles or the other security guard. He went right to Big Cat Country.

There were two different habitats for the big cats, one for the lions and one for the tigers. Both had big fences and a dirty moat between the people and the cats, and as much as he wanted to climb over that fence and lie with those cats, he knew it wasn't possible. Instead, he went to the wolf habitat. There was a fence around it as well but no moat.

Grabbing the links of the fence with his thin fingers, he pulled himself up, not caring if he was being foolish or brave, and dropped to the other side. The wolves didn't have an indoor area to go to, they were outside all day and night, and he was in there, with them.

There were four gray wolves in the exhibit, one of which had been born in the zoo. Trigger had helped feed them a few times and went to clean up their shit a few other times, but he didn't have much interaction with them apart from that. Smiley said they were socialized and used to people but still had instincts that made them dangerous. Like people, he supposed.

There was only one night in the zoo Trigger could remember hearing them crying out, howling. Of all the nights he stayed there, only once. He pictured them, necks craned up, the moon commanding them to pray, but Smiley said that was a myth. He said they howled to show the size of their pack, or to prepare for a hunt, or if one was lost. If one got lost, it would call the others and they would respond, leading it back to the safety of the pack.

Trigger crawled behind one of the huge fiberglass rocks and prepared himself to try again to fall sleep. It wasn't a safe spot like with the tortoises or the elephants or even the African exhibit. Here they could easily get to him if they wanted to, but he really didn't care, and he felt no fear. He lay behind that rock, backpack pillow, looking up at the moon and all of the souls of the city between him and it. The moon, totally full and as bright and fluorescent as if it were plugged in. Like a switch could be hit and it would go dim, dying to a pinpoint in the center before turning complete gray. A freshly cleaned, perfectly round white dinner plate glued up there in the black sky. It hung unconcerned, oblivious to the struggles and hungers of the animals down on Earth, and Trigger realized the man was right. The Rasta with the burning eyes was right. That moon was as much his as any other being that could see it that night. As much his as someone in some far-off country he would never get to, or some animal hunting beneath it in the desert.

Trigger howled out loud, at first just lightly to himself, then stronger and louder. So loud he wanted every one of those burned-up children on Osage Avenue to hear him. So loud he knew Myles and any other person in that zoo would hear him. He howled until he was crying. Then the answer. Each of those wolves howled back, letting him know they were there. Each one of them was looking for him, leading him back to the safety of the pack. The wolves in that fenced-in pen in that zoo in the middle of Philadelphia were concerned about him. He felt perfectly safe, safer than he had felt almost his entire life.

He felt more at home inside that zoo than anyplace else he had ever lived.

☙

The glass showered down, and that screaming drilled right into his head, except this time there was something different. The scream was higher, closer. It rattled his chest and hurt from the inside out. He realized, for the first time, his mother wasn't the only one screaming. It was him. He was screaming the loudest. Sharon's spine had broken, her cord severed, and his mother caught, flailing with all she had, trying to escape the flames clawing at her feet and legs, but it was him, the one with the small cut on his head, he was the one screaming. As loud as a fox in the night, like a murder. He was the one.

☙

Rabbit rabbit.

A rabbit among wolves.

He walked right by two of the wolves. It was early, the sun just risen, and he could still see the pale moon fading, losing the battle to the orange-hot morning. He walked out from behind the rock, and the two wolves were standing right in front of him, heads low but eyes up. Trigger didn't back away, didn't run. He walked right by them. Their gray and white fur matted with sleep, they sniffed the scent that rolled off him, the strange, new scent they had been curious about all night. They didn't show teeth, he was one of the pack and they knew it.

That was the last night he ever slept in the zoo.

⁂

He spent that whole next day as a lone wolf, hunting and exploring. It was a Saturday, a day Smiley would have had him working, but Rob didn't have him scheduled. He had almost three hundred dollars on him, all the money he had left from working all summer, and he ate what he wanted and drank what he wanted. That night he returned to the zoo ready to settle down with his pack again, but he didn't have the chance. The fence had been patched. More than that, it was reinforced with rebar driven deep into the earth. He shook and clawed at it, begging to get in, but he couldn't get the rebar loose. He howled at the heavy clouds in the sky but got no answer. He was truly homeless now, no pack to sleep with or den to sleep in.

His fingers held onto that cold fence, clinging to an idea that dissipated like smoke. The clouds opened up, and it started to pour down, cooling the anger that still drifted from Osage Avenue. Razor wire sat at the top of the zoo's fence, and he figured he could get across if he really tried, but that would just be for tonight, and there was night after night to think about now. His nights at the zoo were over. It was all over. That part of his life was gone, and he knew it.

He let go of the fence and never once again stepped back into the Philadelphia Zoo. Not to sleep, work, or visit.

The rain pelted down, and he needed to find shelter like the rest of the animals. He remembered the graffiti-covered concrete caves beneath Zoological Drive. The 34th Street bridge was so close he could see it, so he squeezed between the chain-link fence gates that divided Zoological Drive from the train tracks and headed for it. He crept alongside the empty spaces beneath the road, peeking into each one, hunched over in the rain. Each was dry with tan earth; cement side and back walls made each seem like an alcove, something you might see in some warped museum dedicated to the hopeless, to the addicted, to the dead. The spaces got larger as Zoological Drive headed uphill toward the bridge. When he got to the last and biggest opening, he crawled into it and sat there with his knees pulled up tight to his chest and his back against the cold cement, holding himself together in a ball. After months of concern and worry and daydreams, he had ended up under that bridge after all.

There were crumpled beer cans and broken bottles in there. A milk crate, some empty soup cans, miscellaneous garbage. And a hubcap with ash in it from the fire he noticed once when crossing by. Someone had spent time in there, maybe still did. He was a trespasser, and he began to feel frightened that someone might return, but the force of the storm kept him there. He'd spent nights out in the rain before. It was uncomfortable, and he knew that it would eventually pass; he just had to hang on until it did. But this was a thunderstorm. A hard-driving, angry thunderstorm that raged for recognition. He had never been outside, even in the zoo, during a driving thunderstorm, and it was terrifying. He was fourteen years old and clinging on to what very little he had, holding onto himself as the world spilled all it could onto him.

After about an hour, he started to nod off, his head dropping onto his knees, when he was suddenly yanked awake. Two of the street dead found him, and they were pulling at his backpack, still strapped over his shoulders. It was a man and a woman; the man was tall and black and in the dark could have passed for Smiley, while she was a white girl, heavy, with stringy wet black hair. She had on a black tank top and was covered with olive green tattoos. They were both soaked and smelled like wet dog.

The woman gritted her teeth as she pulled at his pack, and her teeth were as stained and splintered as Bob's or Sharon's. Trigger tucked his elbows in to lock the backpack into his body, but she kept pulling. The man reached down to break his hold, and as he leaned into Trigger, he could see a tattoo on his taut black neck, it said JESUS. As she pulled Trigger around, he tried to get to his feet but only got as far as his knees when the man punched him hard on the side of the head, just at the temple. The man held a piece of solid metal in his hand, and Trigger's head rang louder than the storm. He tried to shake it off, but the man struck him again, just as hard, and Trigger dropped, groggy and panting, in the dirt.

He could feel them, their filthy hands digging into his jean pockets, and he could still hear them talking to each other about what he had. About what they wanted. They turned his front pockets inside out but found only a few dollars and the yellow change purse. So they took everything else, including his backpack. All his money was hidden in the strap of that backpack. Then the man was saying he wanted his pants, and the two of them pulled his jeans down to his feet, but they got hung up on Trigger's worn sneakers. They kept tugging, violently, dragging him across the loose earth, but the pants wouldn't come off. Then Trigger felt hands pressing into his pale white ass cheeks, spreading them. He was awake enough to know what was going on but dazed enough not to be able to do anything about it. With one dizzy eye, he could barely make out the woman digging into his backpack and pulling everything out, feeling each piece with her grubby, smoke-stained fingers. Then a shock up his spine as he felt something long and hard slide into his asshole. It was probing, feeling around, and he groggily squirmed on the ground, crawling like a worm washed out by the rain. It was pulled out and he felt relief, then the real pain came. The man had jammed his finger in just to find his way in the dark, and once he found the opening, he crammed his penis in with so much venom and force Trigger was sure he'd been ripped apart.

He screamed a terrible scream of pain, so pitiful that any animal in the jungle would have stopped out of mercy, a shrill screech that almost rose above the storm and made its way into that zoo. He imagined every animal hearing him, all howling and stamping and roaring. The elephants throwing up their trunks and blowing their trumpets, pacing desperately to find a way out, to tear down the fencing and stomp that man to death. The wolves gathering, hunting for a way to escape, to protect one of their own. But they couldn't. None of them could.

The dead man jammed it in, again and again. No moral consequences. Dry and grinding, slow, then pounding fast. Trigger was watching the woman put all of his things back in the backpack as her partner went at it. She was right there, allowed it to happen, only concerned with herself. It was like they were two different species at war. And it seemed they were. At one point, the man struck Trigger on the back of the head again, and Trigger saw that white flash and struggled to stay awake. He was already completely prone, humiliated and helpless, and yet he was struck again, for no reason.

He heard groaning and whimpering, the same kind he had heard more than once coming from Sharon's room, and realized he was the one making the sounds. He was a victim of the dead, just as Sharon was, under that bridge in the rain, outside of the zoo and away from his family. A wounded animal, left to the mercy of others, and hoping for reason and empathy, hoping their instincts would kick in and realize they were attacking one of their own kind. But they weren't the same kind, he knew. Not really.

What happened under that bridge perhaps solidified what Trigger had already begun to accept, that maybe we should all live by Natural Law, the real law. The only law.

When the man finished, Trigger was left there, pants still down around his ankles and face in the dirt, crying so hard the tears ran from down his face into the dirt, creating tiny mud puddles on the ground. His attackers took his pack and left, not caring if he was in agony, or crippled, or dead. He lay there for a lifetime, ten thousand lifetimes, naked and exposed to the world, face in dirt created eons ago.

Finally he sat up but was in so much pain he could hardly move. He managed to get his pants up and stumbled out onto the railroad tracks, back into the driving sheets of rain, back onto Zoological Drive. The trees in the zoo leaned their shoulders into the same wind he pushed against. It felt like every stinging drop from the sky landed on his face. They took his backpack and everything in it, every dollar he had. The whole summer of work, all his possessions, gone, simply because someone else wanted them. Even the change purse that had held the key. Even the note from Smiley. But he remembered what Smiley had written on it: Covenant House of Pennsylvania. Right in North Philly.

## Sixteen

IT WAS HOT BUT NOT THE UNTAMED HEAT FROM a flame. It was comforting. Protective. An embracing warmth from the sun overhead behind a few high clouds; big palm leaves against the blue sky. There was no past, only the clear sky and the sun, and the earthy, familiar smell of the hay and the animals.

⁂

Rabbit rabbit.

⁂

Something was different this morning.

The sheets were dry and heavily starched, with a smell of strong detergent. White, with a thin brown scratchy blanket on top. Most people would have found a reason to complain, but he was content to stay under that blanket forever. There were two bunk beds in the room, and he, being the newest, had the bottom bunk nearest the door, and that was fine too. It was regimented. No sleeping in or coming in late. There was order; people were making an effort.

Trigger had been there since the night of the rape, just over two weeks. He'd staggered out from that cave and floated down the street in the pouring rain, drifting like a twig at the mercy of a river, walking down 34th Street, stiff and soaked. He waddled from side to side. Couldn't bend his knees, and with each step, he cried so hard and so loud he could have sworn the whole universe heard him, but the summer storm just swallowed the sound.

Animals don't cry, he knew. Yes, they can show emotion, but humanity is the only species that allows the display of such weakness. Crying has no benefit except to show others your pain; in the animal kingdom, that can never be allowed. In the human kingdom, it rarely helps either.

By the time that police car had rolled up beside him, Trigger was soaked so deeply that the rain had just about drowned out the fire he had been feeling all summer. They asked some questions he would never remember. Trigger did manage to ask the officer to take him to the Covenant House. He was dropped off a total mess, a new animal from the wild coming into a new kind of zoo. Trigger never got the officer's name.

After checking him over, they sent him right to the hospital to get stitched up. A few days later, he was back. There was breakfast and dinner, and Trigger worked cleanup crew. He was given a caseworker, a woman named Katie, who listened to his story as she waited patiently for him to open up. Middle-aged, with a kind, round face and soft hands, she eased his nerves those first few days, and he found out he had nothing to fear. Everyone was there to help. Even the other kids were kind to him and helped him adjust. It was a collaborative effort, aiming for the betterment of all, the opposite of what he was used to, and each moment that passed, he felt better. More trusting. More hopeful.

There were classes and programs. Educational, psychological, and spiritual, all intended to serve as a beacon, an anchor. There were kids there his age, some older, and some younger. Some were disturbed and as angry as that Rasta with the bullhorn, seemingly unreachable, suffering from real-life traumas these kids should have been too young to know about. Prostitution, neglect, addiction. Trigger began to realize maybe he wasn't so alone.

Others had found peace and had already let go of their pasts, had glued themselves back together, the cracks and scars healed over, though still shiny and visible. There were ex-gang members looking for a safe place to lay low, fearing retribution; young girls who were forced into prostitution; run-aways; junkies; and kids like him, just abandoned. The forgotten.

The building was just off a commercial strip in North Philadelphia, not too far from where Smiley had lived. There was a simple sign outside that said, *Covenant House Pennsylvania, Opening Doors for Homeless Youth*. With over twenty locations throughout the United States, they had been helping lost kids since the early 1970s. It was a strict place. No cursing. Shirts tucked in, and no pants hanging down off your ass. The rules were exacting, and breaking them meant you were out. But they had freedoms, times when you could come and go as you wanted—as long as you were back by curfew.

One of the kids in his room was a member of the same gang Will and Troy were in. He was a few years older than Trigger and wore a light trench coat and a hard, felt-covered black bowler hat even though it was still blazing hot out. After he found out they were from the same neighborhood and that they knew a few of the same people, he opened up some. The kid knew both Will and Troy Thomas. He told Trigger that Will had survived and was downtown at Hahnemann Hospital. He said he didn't know who'd shot him but said it with a grin. Will had been selling Bob's meth on his own and cutting out the gang, keeping the profits for himself, and the shooting was payback. Will didn't name the shooter, and neither did Trigger.

Although he was feeling much better and overall more positive about things, Trigger still could not shake the image of Sharon trapped in Bob's house. Sharon was now his only connection to anything. Smiley was gone, off to San Diego to try and create a new future, to forge his own fate. Trigger still felt hurt by his leaving but was beginning to understand and accept it, like a lot of things that were beyond his control. The zoo was closed to him. Trigger could no longer stay there, and he no longer worked there. He didn't want to do either any longer.

He saw one kid in a wheelchair at the Covenant House, and it motivated him to try again at getting Sharon out from under Bob's rule. If they were both there, together, away from Bob and meth and Osage Avenue, things would be different, he thought. He just needed to heal a bit.

After about a month of showers and beds and meals, Trigger was as physically strong and healthy as he could ever remember. Through therapy and counseling, he was better adjusted mentally. He exercised each morning with other kids and continued working with Katie, who convinced him to be good to himself. To forgive himself, as well as others. He began to see things a bit differently, lighter and more positively. If a new kid came in, Trigger would be the first one there to say hello and show him around. His head began to clear. Everything he did, he did with enthusiasm. Not everything was gray and covered in ash anymore. But still, he couldn't live with the fact that Sharon was still in that house. He wanted to see Sharon and get her out.

❦

The walk from the Covenant House to West Philadelphia was close to two hours, but he didn't mind. He had once used walking only to fill the days and nights, but now he was beginning to enjoy it. He took his time, soaking in the sounds and feeling the strong rays of the sun; it felt good on his skin. Even though it was the end of summer, the air that once felt oppressive to him now tasted light and sweet. He walked by the zoo and smelled the hay and heard the people, felt the animals calling to him, as if they were checking on him. He was on the outside now, knowing it was a new, big scary world, having lived only inside his cage, having only whatever his keeper gave him. He could feel he was on the precipice of a new life, frightening and exciting and full of possibilities, just like Smiley.

This new feeling followed him like a shadow. The spirits of the street that had swarmed around him all summer were now just a thin whisper. They no longer carried him back to Osage Avenue; he went there instead under his own power.

He sat on the stoop across the street, staring into the empty lot. He had spent hours there that summer, looking into that lot, believing in MOVE's motives—or at least wanting to believe—but now another voice was in his head, not the voice forced in by the loudspeaker that was once mounted on the side of the house but a voice he let in. He began to try rationalizing what had happened. Was MOVE right in their dissension, or were they just perpetuating a problem that they themselves had caused? Was John Africa truly a leader, a visionary, or just a man with charisma who seduced others to his way? He didn't have all the answers, but he knew that his neighborhood was never going to be the same. The people of Philadelphia were never going to be the same. He was never going to be the same. Right or wrong, they had been (and still were) committed to their cause, and that took strength, courage, to stand alone. They'd fought hard for what they believed was right, and he was going to do the same. Maybe some of the ash from the fire that night got into his blood, and it pumped through his body still. He slapped his palms on his knees and got up to go to Bob's.

It was the last time he looked in at the MOVE house, the last time he felt the need to.

He turned and headed back toward the house. He wasn't exactly sure what time it was, but the faint sliver of pale moon in the dusky sky meant he had to get back to the Covenant House soon or he would be locked out for not making curfew.

He decided he wasn't going back alone.

The closer he got to Bob's house, the harder his heart pumped. He wanted to slow down, he wanted to walk right past and instead get back to that bed with those clean sheets, but his instinct pushed him to try and do the right thing, a drive beyond his control. Protect the pack at all costs. So his legs dragged him on, right to that maroon van in the street. On the stoop sat one of the stoned dead, and at just fourteen years old Trigger felt at least three times his size. He could have stepped from the sidewalk right onto the porch in one massive step if he'd wanted; instead he bounded up the stoop as lightly as a bird hopping from branch to branch. The door gave its creak as he pushed it open, a familiar but distant memory. No one was on the couch. The deadbolt on the basement door was slid open, with that heavy brass lock sitting next to the stuffed ashtray. Bob was down there.

Up the dark-stained steps he pulled himself forward by the rail. The first thing he noticed was the bathroom. No door. And in the doorway to Sharon's room, the trim that he had previously ripped off had been haphazardly nailed back on. Sharon was on the bed, wearing a white T-shirt, her back to the door, lying in the fetal position. Trigger crept in, wanting to get as close to her as he could without her knowing he was there. Wanting to see her undisturbed, in her sadly natural environment, not wanting to spook her. As the floor groaned, he froze and she lifted her head, still not facing him. He took another step, and the floor groaned again.

"You shouldn't have come back," she said without looking toward him. She laid her head on the yellowed, coverless pillow.

"How did you know it was me?"

She took a deep breath in, and her lungs softly rattled.

"Anyone who comes in this room doesn't do it quietly." The room seemed bigger and she seemed smaller. Something was different, then he realized her wheelchair was missing.

"Where's your chair?"

"Bob took it. Took it into the basement. Says I don't need it no more."

With that she rolled over. Her ghostly legs lagged behind as her upper body twisted. Trigger had seen injured animals in the zoo, even animals that were close to death, but seeing her twist this way was the most frightening and disturbing movement he had ever seen. Her face was sallow, almost translucent. Pocked with scabs over broken scabs. Her hair was dry and brittle, as dead and limp as her legs. It hung across her face and eyes, twisted and tangled, with knots that were the beginnings of unintentional dreadlocks. She looked at the wall behind him, through him, like a soldier looking over a burned-out battlefield. She pushed that straw hair away from her face with slender fingers, bone covered in thin paper, long nails with the skin drawn back, like a vampire that had been resting in its crypt for eons. The backs of her hands were more scabbed than her face, with fresh blood between her thumb and palm.

Trigger caught himself drawing back and turning his head, peeking at her from just the corners of his eyes, like seeing a terrifying scene in a movie but not wanting to look away. She propped herself up on one fragile elbow and rested her lollipop head in the palm of her hand. "You should go," she said again. "There's nothing here for you. And if Bob sees you, he says you won't be leaving here."

He sat on the bed, and the slight weight was enough to cause her to dip forward.

"I'm gonna go," he said, "but your gonna come with me."

Trigger told her about the Covenant House, about how they could go there together. How things could change and how she could be free, out of captivity. He expected her to be excited, to at least nod or consider the possibility. But she just laid her head back on that flat pillow and stared into the faded ceiling of the only universe she knew.

"It's too late," she said.

"No, it's not. We can go. We can do it this week."

"No," she said. "You can. I can't." She rolled back over into her fetal position, her bony spine to him. "We're moving. Bob is making some big deal, one big deal, then we're moving. That's why he got that van, to pack us up and get out of here. I think he's got some people after him or something. He's moving and he's taking me with him. Me and my disability checks." She took a deep breath in, her thin frame expanding and her lungs wheezing. "I don't even care," she blew out.

"Moving?" his shoulders slumped forward and he stared into that dark hardwood floor.

"Okay, then we'll go tonight. Right now."

"He'll get us. He'll find me and get me."

"It's safe there. He won't know where we are."

She rolled back over with a heavy sigh, seemingly using all of what little energy she had. She lay there quietly for a few seconds, thin chest pushing up and down. "How? He's got my chair. I can't even leave this room. Even if we do go, he knows people. He'll find me."

Trigger dug his fingers into the filthy mattress and shook his head. He could feel the memory of the heat from Osage Avenue, the heat from the fire, from the car. That little ember had turned into an inferno. He stood up, and she popped back with the bounce of the springs beneath her.

"We're going."

"Wait," she said. "I know why you want to do this. Why you think you need to do this." She reached her skeleton hand out and held his. "It wasn't your fault. The accident. It was just that, an accident. Things happen. You were just a little kid. It's not your fault that I'm here. I make my own decisions too, you know. You're not the only one who has things to deal with. Leave and don't come back."

It was something Trigger had wanted to hear from her his whole life. From anyone, and it gave him more steam to do what he went there for in the first place.

He pulled his hand back sharply.

Trigger left the room and stomped down the steps, not creeping, not on the balls of his feet, each step reverberating through the entire city, as if he wanted everyone to know where he was going. The vibrations surrounded him, wavering out across the room and into the street, across all of Philadelphia.

He swung the basement door open and clanged down the steps like he was eight feet tall and made of steel. The fluorescent light cloaked him, along with the smell of ammonia and paint thinner. He crashed his way down until he stood at the bottom of the steps, in the full light of the lab, not a shadow on him. Halfway into the room, in front of the table with the jars and bottles and propane and thinner, was Bob, shirtless, with a respirator pulled up onto his head, flattening out his wiry hair. His face was sweaty and streaked red where the straps had wrapped him just a few seconds earlier. The key dangled from his neck. His hands were tight across the barrel and stock of his shotgun, pointing it toward the intruder and eyeing down the site.

When Bob saw who it was, he lowered the shotgun and snickered, then flopped the barrel across the clammy skin of his shoulder with a slap, holding the gun from the bottom of the butt. There was a large tray of crystal on the table in front of him, large chunks that he hadn't broken up yet. He pulled out one of the smaller shards and crushed it with the back of a spoon on the table, balancing the gun at the same time. He bent down and snorted it up without holding a finger to his other nostril, then stood back up, eyes watery and ablaze.

"So you couldn't stay away. Just . . . just had to come back."

Behind him on the far side of the room was Sharon's wheelchair, brown leather and black tires creased with age.

"I just want to get her chair," Trigger said. "I just wanna get her chair, then we're gone."

"We? Whadda you mean *we*?

Bob turned his back, and the black steel of the barrel poking up over his shoulder kept an eye on the room. With his free hand, he pulled the wheelchair over and flopped into it. He was on the far side of the table, and Trigger was still near the stairs, about eight feet of drug paraphernalia between them. Bob sat in the chair and spun it to face him, the shotgun straddled across the armrests as his arms lay across the gun.

"She ain't goin' nowhere. No . . . nowhere. I told you that." He was jittery and tweaked, scratched feverishly at a scab on his arm and, without looking up, continued. "Either are you. I told you not to come back here. I did . . . told you. I was serious. But here you are. Trigger. Come back to save the day." He rambled on a bit more, but it was garbled gibberish, like he was speaking only to himself. He nodded in response to his own words, but he was the only one understanding what he said.

Trigger took a few steps toward him, running his hand across the table. A propane bottle sat on the floor, and he nudged it out of the way with his foot, then cleared some of the empty cold pill cartons away.

"This ain't right," he said, shaking his head. "It ain't right what you're doing. None of this is normal."

"Normal? Right? What do you know about normal and right?"

"I know this ain't right. You keep your daughter locked up. You have sex with your own daughter. You're sick. You're a sick bastard. Have sex with your daughter and try to kill your son. You're not right in the head. You fried your brain."

Bob shifted the gun and pointed it straight up toward the open framing of the basement ceiling, tangled with wires and exhaust venting and the dust of lives before. He sat the butt in his crotch. Again he spoke a broken jumble of words, words that he seemed to understand but no one else ever would. The language of the dead. The babbling of the junkie who doesn't realize he is a junkie. He broke the conversation with himself to address Trigger again.

"You, you don't know a goddamn thing," he said. "You don't know . . . no goddamn clue what you're talking about."

Trigger took two more steps forward and slammed his hand on the table. His hand that for so long seemed thin and powerless to him, now seemed as strong as Smiley's.

Bottles rattled.

"I don't know?" he yelled. "I know more than anybody what you're doing in here. You're just a slimy drug dealer, a junkie, a little spider down in your hole here, hiding out from the real world. Keeping your daughter as a slave, a sex slave. Incest, that's what that's called. It ain't right. I'm taking that chair and she's coming with me. You can do whatever you want after that, but that's gonna be it."

Bob shook his head at the ceiling and mumbled some more.

"Mother . . . mother, just like. You're just like your mother. Ungrateful . . . ungrateful for everything I gave you."

Trigger's mouth opened, waiting for words to fall out, but it took a few seconds before they could get from his brain to his throat.

"Everything you gave me?" he yelled. "You? Gave me? What did you ever give me? Or Sharon? Either of us?"

"A roof, a bed to sleep in." Bob dropped his head down and scratched around the wood butt of the gun with his finger, fidgeting, and craned his neck from side to side. "I gave you everything you needed. Everything . . ." He trailed off again, then focused back in. "What you do with it is up to you."

Trigger stood dumbfounded for a moment by Bob's explanation, and he again struggled to find the right words. But he realized he was not dealing with a stable person. A sane person. He was hardly a person at all in Trigger's eyes.

"You gave us nothing. We're your children. This is no way to treat animals, let alone kids. You're no kind of father. You're a horrible father. A horrible person."

Bob dropped the cold barrel of the shotgun into his other hand and pointed it lazily at Trigger, the butt still dug into his crotch. He twitched and shook, fighting the urge to scratch at his skin, but the compulsion was beyond his control.

"No kind of father," he said. His eyes rolled wildly. "That much you're right about. No . . . no kind of father. In fact, I'm not a father at all. At least not to you. Or her. I had one kid, and he was taken away from me."

Trigger took a step back, the shotgun still pointed at his stomach, unsure of what Bob meant. He waited to see if he would continue. He did.

"Didn't know that, did you Mr. Know-it-all? That's right, that's it. I'm not your father. Or Sharon's."

Trigger squinted his eyes at him so hard he could barely see through the humming white light. He figured Bob was just trying to get a reaction from him.

"What are you talking about?" Trigger rocked back on his heels for just a moment, keeping his eyes on the shotgun in Bob's lap. "You're full of shit."

"Oh, am I?" Bob smiled, as if he was about to lay down a winning hand of cards on the table and wanted to take his time doing it. He pulled his feet from the floor into the footrests on the chair and let out a large sigh, relaxed and confident. "You don't know anything. Your real daddy wanted you aborted. That's right. Sucked out, but your mamma wouldn't do it. Sucked . . . out. An' when you got closer to bein' born, he figured he'd juss take care of it himself . . . *TRIGGER*," he said, drawing out the name like it was the first time he had ever heard the word. He smiled again, a brown, gaping mouth.

"After he beat the shit out of her, he split. Gone forever. Sharon, she . . . she didn't even know him; she was just a baby. So me being the solid guy I was, when I got involved with your mom, I played house. Played the daddy. Then she up and died. Died 'cause of you." He shook his head and sniffed, trying to settle his thoughts. Focusing hard on trying to form complete sentences. "That's right, too. Didn't think I knew that either, I guess. Sharon told me all about it, all about how it was you. It was you caused that accident that killed her. Left you two with no one. So I stepped up. I stepped up and gave you a roof and a bed, even after you fucked everything up. Sounds like I'm a real horrible person, don't it?"

Trigger took another step back, almost to the steps.

"I don't believe you."

"That's fine, believe what you want. But a fact is a fact." He rambled on about how a fact was a fact, his wild eyes scanning from the ceiling to the table, then to the steps. He seemed distracted by everything in the room, and his neck jerked from place to place. He fidgeted and adjusted his sweaty grip on the gun, clammy hands clenching.

Trigger tried to figure it all out quickly, but it was too much too fast, and thoughts of the car crash came rolling in, fogging any clarity. That gun was still pointing right at him, held by those shaky hands.

"Even if you're tellin' the truth, it don't make it right. It don't make any of this right. It don't mean you can do that to Sharon."

It took a few seconds for the words to cut through and reach Bob, and when it did, he chuckled out loud, a sound Trigger rarely heard from him. Bob's lips spread open and the brown death in his mouth gaped like a stinking cave.

"You really are a dumb little fuck, ain't you," he said. "Maybe she's not as helpless as you think. What makes you so sure she don't want it this way?"

That made Trigger's blood boil, and he felt a heat in his core that spread out through his veins and into his extremities. His eyes must have glowed as red as the Rasta's, as fiercely as John Africa's or the howling wolves. His hands coiled into bony fists and his lips drew down, sneering and exposing his canine teeth, nose crinkled and eyes alive. He went to lunge at Bob like that tiger pouncing on its slab of meat. Two quick steps. Right there, just two paces in from the steps, what had been simmering for the entire summer, seemingly his entire life, all boiled over.

Bob moved to fire. Trigger saw it and froze, just two steps in, and his hands unlocked, and he turned his head and clasped his eyes tight.

Nothing. Not a sound. Not a click. Not a pop. His ears weren't ringing.

In that split second, the entire cosmos froze, and Trigger was at the exact center again, with all the time in eternity to consider if Bob really meant to kill him. The man was so tweaked, and his hands so shaky and tense, it was possible he had just spasmed, that it was beyond his control, and it had shocked Bob as much as it had shocked Trigger. And that is what Trigger wanted to believe. But he wasn't sure he did. Not quite.

He peeked out of the corner of his eye toward Bob, who looked just as surprised. Bob dropped the barrel to the floor, finger still tight to the trigger and the butt still pressed into his crotch, and looked at the stock, confused by why the trigger had locked solid.

"Safety," he said, and muttered a few more words about being safe. He pushed the safety button forward.

Trigger didn't know if he felt it first or heard it first. When Bob flicked that safety button off, he was so jacked, so tweaked, and his finger still so tight to that trigger that he pulled it. He pulled it, and it kicked him back. He and the wheelchair jolted back as one; he had not braced for the kickback, and the chair's wheels were not locked. The smooth stock of the gun smashed right into his balls, crushing them useless. The barrel of the gun had been pointed slightly toward the floor, and when it went off, it sprayed that buckshot right into one of the propane tanks under the table. It blew, igniting the thinner and the propane bottles in a single hot blast, creating a fireball that threw Trigger back against the far wall by the basement steps. He could feel the scorching hot air billow across his face, singeing his eyebrows. His wispy hair caught the edge as well, the blast frying the ends and blowing it straight back. He was so close, the explosion felt as loud and as powerful as a bomb. Like the bomb that fell on Osage Avenue.

Bob was engulfed, unable to rise from the wheelchair, and the thinner shot all over him and the room and onto the dusty dry beams and floorboards above them. The flash was bright enough to temporarily blind Trigger, but he could hear Bob screaming. Trigger felt his way up the stairs, led mostly by fear and memory. By the time he reached the top, the basement was a river of fire, and he heard another small explosion. Out of instinct he threw the door shut behind him, trying to keep the fire contained to the basement. The smoke was already getting thick in the living room, and licks of fire were working their way up through the kiln-dried hardwood flooring.

He rubbed the palms of his hands into his eyes to clear them, but his vision remained blurry. He could hear Sharon screaming, just like in that fiery car. Her voice shrill and panicked. She was shouting to him, but he didn't hear words, just the wild sounds of her screams. He went to run up the stairs for her, but before he did, he turned back to the basement door and slid the heavy deadbolt into place, locking Bob down there. Locking him into that fire just like his mother had been locked into that front seat. Forging Bob's destiny.

By the time he made it upstairs and had Sharon strapped across his back, the fire had burnt its way through the floor in the living room in several areas. He couldn't feel his feet to know if he had stumbled or jumped, or if the spirits of the dead carried them, but he made it down with her on his back. The smoke was already getting thick and black, and he choked on it as he tripped his way past the basement door.

He couldn't be positive, but he thought maybe he heard Bob—after crawling to those stairs, his skin peeled off and wiry hair burnt to the scalp, then pulling himself up each scalding tread—banging on that door and calling for help. He thought maybe he heard a faint voice, muffled by the smoke and his own rage, asking for mercy.

But it didn't really matter. He was down there one way or another.

Though Bob's lungs and throat must have already been burnt, Trigger imagined he heard him, and not faintly, but as loud as that bomb that dropped on Osage Avenue, as loud as the sirens that followed. He may have possibly heard the meaty part of Bob's fist banging on the faded wood panel of that door where it would leave bloody splotches, each bang thumping in Trigger's chest. He thought maybe he heard Bob screaming as loud and panicked as his mother had, uselessly fighting the flames. Whether Sharon heard anything or not, Trigger never found out, and he never would ask, but to Trigger, the sounds were as the howls he let loose not many nights earlier, when those wolves heard him howl alone in that calm night air.

Trigger carried Sharon out of the house on his sweaty back, the street dead who had been on the front step earlier nowhere to be found. He had likely taken off at the first sign of danger, not bothering to check inside to see if anyone needed help.

Trigger took her to the other side of the street, past the maroon van that Bob was planning to use to escape with Sharon. He sat her on Dottie's concrete stoop and flopped next to her. From the outside, the signs the house was burning up were barely beginning; it was still just another dark house in the middle of a row of dark homes on that dark street, burning only from the lives of the people within.

A few minutes later, smoke started pouring out the front door and flames licked into visibility. People from the houses on both sides came out yelling to one another. After that it seemed only seconds before the house blazed.

The door on the porch opened, and Dottie came out. "Oh my God!" she said, covering her mouth with her frail hand. "I gotta call 911!" She shambled back into the house as fast as her tired old legs could take her.

When she came out again, she noticed a cut on Trigger's face, one he didn't even know he had, so she went back in once more and returned with a Band-Aid, cleaned the cut up gently with a towel and water, and softly put it over his cut. She gently dabbed his face, reddened and tender, then wiped his singed eyebrows and pushed back the hair from his eyes with her soft, thin fingers. It was almost peaceful, almost comforting to him, and it took the breaking of glass to snap him back into what was happening across the street.

The fire blew out the glass of his front bedroom window, and the flames jumped out of the window to their freedom, reaching up onto the roof, into the sky, clawing at the beautiful, indifferent pale moon.

Trigger could hear the house groan as it burned alive, and the spirits of Osage Avenue heard it too, and it led them to the street where they gathered by the thousands to feel the heat and wait for the new arrival. They were drawn to the heat, to the newly dead, as close to the living as they could get.

The living continued gathering. People stood on their front stoops or in the street to watch and worry, pointing and talking. Some were muttering about another bombing, others about whether the fire would spread like the one on Osage Avenue had, and wondering if the fire trucks would stand idly. Again.

By the time Trigger heard the sirens, there were probably fifty people in that street, watching helplessly as the flames scaled the walls from house to house. Trigger noticed the boy with the basketball and the afro, still bouncing the ball as he shook his head at the fire. Dottie was on the sidewalk, leaning in with other older neighbors, hands on their faces. She started to cry.

"Goddammit!" someone yelled. "Every damn thing in my house gonna burn up. Son of a bitch! Where the fire trucks now, when you need them! The whole damn block gonna burn up again! What the hell is goin' on around here?"

Thick black smoke rolled into the sky, blotting out the moon and dropping ash on them like summer snow. In that ash was Bob's soul, now just another of the spirits cursed to wander these same streets, forever feeling the heat of that fire. Just like the MOVE family and all of the dead of West Philadelphia. But not Trigger.

Just before the fire truck squeezed down that narrow street and parted the ocean of people, Trigger saw him. The man outside of the zoo, the Rasta with the red eyes who had been yelling into the bullhorn. He saw that rainbow cap, seemingly above it all, like he knew this was going to happen. He was staring into the flames like the rest of them but wasn't one of them. Trigger was drawn to him, and he left Sharon on the cool stoop and drifted his way through the crowd to stand beside him. They stood shoulder to shoulder, watching the fire burn Trigger's past, black as charcoal. There was a haze of chatter beneath the crackling of the fire and the busting of glass, a hum of accusations and despair. Everyone in the crowd talked at once, some angry, some crying, some even laughing, but the two of them stood in that swirling firestorm in complete silence, each knowing the other was there but not acknowledging each other, just watching that fire consume as much as it wanted, moving as freely as it wanted. The Rasta was shirtless and sweaty, and Trigger could smell him, smell him beneath the smoke and the stink of the city, bitter and stale and refusing to wash the scent off for anyone. The fresh scabs of Osage Avenue, still nearly raw from the MOVE bombing, were torn off, and they were all reminded again that fate drives us where it wants and that freedom is vague and means something different to everyone.

As that first fire truck lumbered down the street, and as the first few people moved out of the way, he finally turned to Trigger, his dreadlocks reaching out in every direction like antennae picking up signals beamed across the universe. His eyes were red and watery, and the flames shone off them like the fire was behind those eyes and burning out at the world.

"Feel that heat? See those flames jumping around?" he asked. "That's Nature doing what it wants. There's no controlling that. Nature's always gonna win out. Can't hold it back. We'll all be gone, and the world will start all over again without us."

The fire truck split the street, and Trigger stepped to the side, away from the fire with everyone else, toward Sharon, and the Rasta was the only one that stepped toward the blaze. He clenched his fist and raised it above his head so they could clearly see its silhouette backlit by the orange flames. He shook it to the sky and shouted so loud Trigger could hear him above the fire truck just yards away.

"Long live John Africa! Long live MOVE!"

Right then the truck pulled between them, blocking Trigger's view of the Rasta, and there was a scramble of firefighters pointing and shouting. Trigger never saw him again. He sat back on the steps with Sharon and watched as the firefighters fought to smother the fire. The fire that was born out of anger and frustration and grew as it consumed, moved as it wanted to move, now dying at the hands of others.

After a few minutes another fire truck made its way down the street. Trigger and Sharon sat on Dottie's stoop, wet with the mist of the hoses and smelling of burnt embers. She offered to let them wait inside, but they wanted to watch the house burn. They sat and watched the flames and the water from the trucks do battle.

The water poured into the basement and finally swallowed the fire and Bob and all of Bob's dreams and everything he hated about himself. Trigger considered Bob's fate and how the man's destiny had been stolen away from him twice, or at least that's what Bob believed, what he couldn't get past. But the whole time he had been heading toward his fate, wide and clean. Straight in front of him, and at the mouth of that river, had been an ocean of opportunity. Instead the stream changed, and he ended up in West Philadelphia, in a basement, and that was where he would remain forever.

The fire destroyed two homes and damaged a third. It was nowhere near the catastrophe the MOVE fire was, but still it uprooted people, and one person—Bob—had died.

❧

Late into the night, the street was taped off and the crowd had almost entirely thinned out. A cop told the two of them to move along, too. When Sharon told the cop they had no place to go, he learned theirs was one of the houses now gone. He took them in his car to the police station, picking Sharon up and gently placing her in the back seat. She was limp, tired, and frazzled, and she poured into the vinyl. Trigger sat beside her in the back of the car and watched out the window as the moon followed them. He couldn't help but think back to the first night he stayed in the zoo, and for some reason, he had that same peaceful feeling he'd had that night. A lot had changed since then but not the moon.

At the police station they were able to find Sharon a wheelchair, newer than hers, with bright chrome and blue leather padding. She sat in it as Trigger took a stiff chair beside an officer's desk. They were asked questions by the officer, but he asked gently and seemed genuinely concerned, even bringing them each a cold soda. Sharon was quiet, and Trigger only answered with yes or no or a head nod. It was no more than a few minutes before the officer rose and told them to wait.

He came back shortly with a woman who said she was going to help them, saying she was a social worker. She led them down a hall, and Trigger pushed Sharon's chair, feeling that if he let go of the handles, he might fall to the floor. It was late, but the hall was bright, and there were pictures on each side of it, framed with proud men in uniforms.

The social worker took them to an office and asked more questions they were both too tired to answer. The office seemed bare, no clutter on the desk, no plants or pictures. Just a desk, some chairs, and a small couch, like she had just moved in that day. She was a kind woman, though barely an adult, probably no more than twenty-two or twenty-three years old, not much older than Sharon. Mocha skin and a round, soft face. Her hair was short and tightly curled, as black as her eyes, and she was dressed in some kind of a suit jacket that didn't look like it fit her, like someone had given it to her just for the job.

Trigger helped Sharon out of the chair, and she laid down on the small couch and fell asleep. He sprawled across a big cloth chair with his legs hanging over the armrests, spent. She asked who, if anyone, had been in the house, and he told her. She asked who they could stay with for the night. He had never really thought about it before, but there wasn't a single person in the whole city that they knew well enough to take them in even for one night, and the only thing he could do about it was rub his sunburnt face with the palms of his hands and chuckle, rather than cry. He could still smell the burnt hair on his head and knuckles, and he lightly touched the Band-Aid on his face, making sure it was still in place. She was tired too and rested her chin in her hands, elbows propped on the desk.

"You have any place you can go? Don't you have anyone that can take care of you?"

He told her he had been staying at the Covenant House, but he thought it was too late in the night to go there. When the words left his mouth, he got nervous. Nervous that maybe he gave her too much information, gave the system too much information, and that information would be used against them. Sharon was still a minor, just as he was, and he figured if they had no one to take care of them, the system would take them away, separate them, put them into foster care. It was the system MOVE fought, the duality of the cosmos, and now Trigger was the one facing it.

All of these things ran though his head, whispering to him to fight, but he pushed them back. There was no one here to fight. If they needed, they could stay at the Covenant House, at least temporarily.

The fight was over. He was free from the zoo. Sharon was free from Bob, and what happened on Osage Avenue would be a constant reminder for the rest of his life: to never take that freedom for granted.

Before he could respond to her questions, she continued.

"Don't you have any family to take care of you?" she shook her head softly.

He thought about that question seriously and didn't rush to answer. He cocked his neck from side to side, took a deep breath in through his nose, held it just a second, then let it out.

"I have an uncle."

⁂

## About the Author

Tony Gervasi grew up in the Philadelphia area and was a teen during the MOVE bombing of 1985. He currently lives in the suburbs of Philadelphia, splitting his time between there and the Florida Keys with his wife and their three dogs. *Osage Avenue* is his first book.

## About the Type

This book is set in Bely, designed by French typeface designer Roxane Gataud in 2012. She describes Bely as "a classy throwback text font family with a fearless and venturesome display."

CPSIA information can be obtained
at www.ICGtesting.com
Printed in the USA
BVHW042208260922
648069BV00003B/20